KEEP THE
CHANGE

Using the 12 Steps to Become a
Better Leader in Every Area of Life

BART NOLLENBERGER

Pat
Love You Brothers!
Thank You!

Bart

PRAISE FOR
KEEP THE CHANGE

Bart Nollenberger's book *Keep the Change* is a wonderful read. It will make a big difference in many lives—that's a guarantee!!
—Pat Williams, NBA hall of famer, co-founder of The Orlando Magic, and author of over 150 books

I have had the opportunity to work closely with Bart for a number of years now, and have seen first-hand the incredible effect of his message. I watched him share his story of overcoming addiction on stage in front of thousands of people and saw the incredible way that it resonates with everyone on some level. You do not have to be an alcoholic or an addict to benefit from Bart's journey! There is something in this book for everyone, because the principles it contains are transformational, universal and timeless.
—Roddy Galbraith, speaker trainer and founder of SpeakerPro

It's here! Bart and I have talked about *Keep the Change* for a few years, as I have been his coach and mentor. Bart is authentic in this book and tells the story of how he got from a place of pain to a place of peace. What I love is that he shows us all how powerful those 12 steps are to being the best we can be as leaders in every area of our life. Do the work and watch your life change. Bart is proof.
—Chris Robinson, executive vice president of Maxwell Entrepreneur Solutions

I met Bart in the mid-nineties at the company we both worked for, Half-A-Car. He was free from alcohol and drugs at that time, but with the knowledge I have gained in the last six years, looking back I would say he was not "sober". Since that time, I have watched him grow into the sincere, dedicated, loving and sober person he is today. Sobriety is not only physical, but mental. The demons don't stop because you are alcohol and drug free. The demons never stop, and Bart has found a way to overpower them. I believe he represents the second part of the serenity prayer, "God grant me the courage to change the things I can." He has truly embodied this phrase and consequently changed many lives, including mine. I treasure his friendship and the fact that I can talk to him with no fear of being judged. Bart helped me through the most difficult time in my life with listening and some very simple compelling words. He said, "God has prepared you for this moment, and out of this tragedy will come something that will last longer than you will." He was correct. God has blessed me in many ways, and Bart's kinship is one of those blessings.

—Frank Marr, Founder of Jake's Reach

The power of and tenderness for Bart's Savior, Jesus, is tangibly felt. Out of his experienced pain and authenticity in sharing with us, he creates space for others to identify areas of brokenness in their own lives and actually see a path forward from victim to victor. We see that peace is within our reach, and there is opportunity for consistent growth that leads to true transformation that keeps the change rather than just behavior modification. Thank you, Bart, for showing us there is hope and that truly, "where we are is a bridge to where we want to be."

—Sarah-Gayle Galbreath, founder of Hope Relentless Marriage and Relationship Center

I first met Bart through mutual friends and soon found out we were kindred spirits. As a pastor of Hope Church in Texas, and Bart as a Celebrate Recovery Leader as well as a background in the same indus-try, we hit it off quickly. I have been on Bart's podcast Keep the Change twice talking about my journey of losing a son and writing a book for those who mourn. Bart's book is a story of courage, one day at a time, and is a must read for all who are leaders in the home, workplace, or in the just struggles of life.

—Will Ramsey, author of *A Father's Journey Through Darkness* and pastor at Hope Church in San Antonio, Texas

I first met Bart in 2013 when I was the President of the John Maxwell team and he became a member. Over the years, he has become a partner and advocate for my work and teachings, but more importantly a friend. I see *Keep the Change* as a journey from a man in distress to a person with victory today in his life at every level. This book will transform you as it obviously did for Bart. Thank you, Bart, for being so bold to share your story.

—Paul Martinelli, founder and past president of the John Maxwell Team, co-founder of the Cialdini Institute for Influence

Keep the Change: Using the 12 Steps to Become a Better Leader in Every Area of Life
by Bart Nollenberger
with Stephen Copeland

www.keepthechangebook.org
www.bartnollenberger.com

Published by The Core Media Group, Inc., www.thecoremediagroup.com.
Cover & Interior Design: Nadia Guy

ISBN 978-1-950465-83-5

Printed in the United States of America.

CONTENTS

This book is dedicated to those who have seen it all—my incredible kids, Tiffany Crocker, Ty Nollenberger, Nick Nollenberger and Dax Nollenberger. You have shown me unconditional love for decades and I am so honored to be your dad. And, to my wife, Mary, who showed me what a true love story looks like. I love you all so much!!

A special acknowledgment to my Momma in Heaven who was my rock and role model. Thank you, despite all I put you through, for always believing in me!! I love you so much and miss you every day!!

And, to my grandparents in heaven, Bessie and Harold Nollenberger. Thank you for your constant prayers and never giving up on me. I am who I am because of your never-ending faith, belief and love.

FOREWORD

This book tells a story, one that has insight into you and your life. You will notice three "cords" woven through Bart's life. Each of us, at some point, will grapple with these cords. The first cord: Jesus is the Ultimate Truth. Bart weaves his faith story throughout these chapters in a way with which you will connect. It is not "churchy", although church is part of it. It is transformational. The second cord: finding practical wisdom for how to successfully live life. Bart has embraced the 12-step program as the tool to implement his life. Millions of people have rebuilt their lives around the wisdom found in the 12 steps. Bart's story will help you find this wisdom. The third cord: finding a life purpose. You will see that Bart's life purpose is to help others find freedom from addiction and ultimately in Jesus. Bart's life purpose has its roots in God redeeming the brokenness of his past.

I know Bart both as a pastor and as a friend. His story is real. I have been in groups with him, watched him love his wife, serve his church, and build a Celebrate Recovery team. Like all of us, Bart's story is still being written. There is wisdom in what he has written. Let Bart challenge you as you read Keep the Change.

Rick Linaman
Co-Founder and President of Unleash God's Dream

INTRODUCTION

Do you want to change something? If you've picked up this book, my guess is that the answer is yes. The fact is, we all have *something* we need to change because we're all addicts in some way. That's right, *addicts*. Think about it. We're all insecure in some way, and therefore every single one of us has voids we try to fill. These insecurities become the very harbors for our addictions—where we tend to fill the void ourselves instead of being formed and transformed by God.

As you pick up this book, you might not be an alcoholic or substance abuser like I was. Maybe your vice is over-eating or pornography or cigarettes or even something you may have never considered an addiction like victimhood, busyness, lethargy, gossip, or attention and affection. Maybe it's technology—*cough, cough*—like your iPhone.

There is no doubt that we live in an age that is rife with distractions and dopamine boosts. All of these things are attempts (often reactive attempts) to fill the voids in our lives. Often times these voids were formed by pain. Without awareness we might venture through our lives reacting to past pain.

To understand our addictions, we have to first understand ourselves.

When I was twenty-eight years old I walked into a rehab facility called the Adrian Center in Santa Cruz, California. I had spent my life unknowingly chasing attention and affection at all costs. Cocaine made me feel confident and invincible on a journey where I continually felt like I wasn't good enough. Alcohol not only numbed my pain but also fed my fantasizing. I longed to be someone other than my broken self.

At the Adrian Center I was first introduced to the 12 Steps of Alcoholics Anonymous. I was arrogant and narcissistic. I could not even say the word "humility" because the concept was so foreign! But slowly, ever so slowly, God transformed me through the 12 Steps. Over the last thirty plus years, as many alcoholics will tell you, addiction tried to take form in new ways, but I am humbled to say that while writing this book I've received over thirty-seven years of freedom from drugs and alcohol. By the grace of God—and only by the grace of God—I write this nearly four decades sober from alcohol and drugs.

The Steps got me on the journey of transformation and continue to transform me today. That is one reason why this book is titled *Keep the Change*. The Steps taught me that change is a lifestyle. Evolution never stops. To keep the change, I believe we must never stop transforming. We must never stop being curious about ourselves and areas in our life where we can grow. In Christianity, this process is called sanctification: being continually conformed into the image of Christ, who modeled selflessness and service. The best leaders I know never arrive. Their curiosity paves the way for continual introspection. They have a grace for themselves that positions them to not be defined by their failures. They see mistakes as opportunities. They govern their lives by what I call the "Laws of Transformation:" self-awareness, integrity, vision, and understanding our why. Every situation, whether success or failure, is an opportunity for transformation.

This is not meant to *just* be a leadership book. But it will certainly apply to people who want to become better leaders, and, frankly, better people. This book contains numerous self-development principles. This is not meant to be a memoir either but will include transparent stories from my own journey through (and with) addiction. The goal in all of this is to invite you into the transformative and liberating nature of self-development—into *true* change so that you can become a better spouse, parent, leader, and steward of the life God has gifted you. With true change comes the ultimate goal, which is peace. True peace comes when you *keep* growing and don't go backwards—when you *keep* the change. If you do the principles and stay with these steps, you'll be a better person and keep the change.

You might be able to tell already that I am unashamed to talk about God and my faith. It is such an integral part of my journey that it would be dishonest to *not* talk about it. But, like the 12 Steps, my hope is that this book is accessible to you, even if you are a staunch atheist. When I walked through those doors at the Adrian Center, I believed in God but had no idea who He was. The Steps transformed me on how I thought about myself and also on a spiritual level, though I did not become a Christian until much later in life. I have found my ultimate hope and peace through Jesus Christ, but you should know from the get-go this book's goal is not to convert you to Christianity. I hope the Scripture I've included stirs your heart. I hope the spiritual principles in this book invite you into authentic change. There is no agenda here but to come alongside you through these words.

This book is broken down into twelve chapters. Each chapter aligns with a step from recovery. As you read, you'll notice that every chapter unfolds on three levels: with a story from my own life, the journey of recovery; with a dissection of the particular step that corresponds with each chapter using biblical principles; and with additional leadership and self-development principles that build upon the particular step and call you into action. The purpose is to show you both the personal and universal application of the Steps. This was the most authentic and truthful structure for this book. The Steps impact me just as much today as they did thirty-seven years ago when I walked into the Adrian Center. In fact, they take on more power the more you live with them. They are truly timeless, fueling curiosity and transformation.

You should know, however, that I was hesitant to write a book. I'm passionate about developing leaders and am a certified John Maxwell coach, Celebrate Recovery ministry leader, and mental health coach, but something about writing a book—laying it all out there—felt too vulnerable to me for a long time. Yes, there is nothing more fulfilling to me than coming alongside someone and helping them use their addiction as a springboard for their own growth, whether it's the young alcoholic taking my sales training course right now or the person I'm sponsoring whose addiction has led him to adopt a very low self-esteem. Yet I always knew that if I chose to write a book, I had to be all in. There was no hiding behind leadership principles or spiritual principles. I had to marry them with my story. I don't think I was ready to do this until very recently. While a lot of my peers are entering retirement, in many ways I am beginning again: reflecting on my six decades of life through this book. In some ways, it is a cautionary tale. I pray you do not make the same mistakes I made. My first three decades of life established patterns that, to this day, are still difficult to break. But, more than anything, I hope this book is human and relatable. I hope it helps you in some way, whether it's one paragraph, chapter, or theme. If it helps one person find peace and freedom from their addiction, this book had done its job.

Out of respect for my family, know that these chapters will not be a play-by-play or tell-all. Yet it is vulnerable enough that it was scary to write. As any addict will tell you, addiction can make you so disoriented and detached. In my "new life" I couldn't believe some of the things I had done. Yet we are to be victors, not victims. We have to carry our baggage with us. Victors take full responsibility and are not defined by their baggage. Victims, on the other hand, blame others. I believe the more vulnerable we each choose to be, the less alone others feel as they navigate their own hurts, habits, and hangups. By the grace of God, I am where I am today, with a brilliant and beautiful wife who accepted me as I was, my past and all. Between the two of us we have ten children and eleven grandchildren. I have a thriving business and am speaking at places I never could have dreamt. I'm now an author. This book is for anybody who wants to get from from a place of pain to a place of victory and peace. This book is for addicts but not *just* for addicts. Reading this book will help you journey through massive pain to victory on the other end. Every human being wants peace. Victory *is* peace. Whether you consider yourself an addict or not, the great thing about this journey is for you to learn about yourself as you develop the skills to love and accept yourself. Growth and change can only happen if you want to.

Consider these words Corinthians 12:2, "But God chose the foolish things of the world to shame the wise; God chose the weak things of the world to shame the strong." This is an upside down gospel narrative. What that means in today's world is that you are learning from an expert who has a master's in stupidity, an expert who knows what door *not* to take. In our social-media-driven world, we are used to creating a curated image of ourselves, but the addict's superpower is vulnerability.

Being a recovering addict myself and constantly learning from addicts in my mentoring, I believe we bear a certain truth about the human condition. For all of us, we want to change something. For addicts who truly want to change, there is no hiding or disguising their insecurity. They must bring it to the surface. They must accept it as their own plight and route to wholeness. Our addictions might make us feel foolish or worthless, but no matter what you've done, you are valued. You have something to offer to others. You might not know it now, but by the end of the book you will know. We all have purpose. Where we are is a bridge to where we want to be. Let's get to work and keep the change, and, by the way, let's have some fun doing it.

As we close this introduction, I'm reminded of what the apostle Paul said in Romans 12:2 (commentary my own): "Do not conform to the pattern of this world (*after all, where has that gotten us?*), but be transformed (*that's my goal for you*) by the renewing of your mind." That's what is going to be so exciting about this journey. The *you* who you are now will not be same person by the time you're done with this book. I want you to get that. Consider reading that sentence again: *The you who you are now will not be same person by the time you're done with this book.* That's what I want for you.

People will notice the difference. You are going to feel fantastic about this as a person, and you are going to start right now. Let's do this.

Scan the QR code to watch a special message from Bart about the Introduction.

CHAPTER 1

PERFUME ON THE PIG

Had I ever felt so good before?

I moved through the crowd at the Bee Hive, struggling to walk straight, my vision beginning to blur. I felt loose and playful, more confident and less self-conscious. All eyes were on me, and I took full advantage of the spotlight—cracking jokes, flirting with girls who were way out of my league, exaggerating my inebriated state by slurring my words. My so-called friends seemed to love this new persona I had crafted (at least I thought so in my mind)—the carefree goofball, loosened by a goblet of whiskey and another of rum. They seemed to laugh with me with a certain adoration in their eyes (really?), as I suddenly received the attention I had always craved. Could they sense my desperation? For once I was "cool," pushing boundaries, entertaining classmates, willing to play the fool so they could laugh.

When I returned home that evening, I was unable to hide my drunken state. At first, my parents were also entertained. I remember them sitting on the edge of my bed, looking at one another and chuckling. But not for long. Sooner or later, my drinking became a point of contention instead of connection.

This sad performance at the Bee Hive, a popular gathering spot for high schoolers in my Ohio hometown, became routine as I struggled my way through high school. I would steal a bottle from my dad's liquor cabinet, poor it in a goblet, and drink much of it on the mile and a half walk to the social stage. When I got my license, my dad gave me a Volkswagen Beatle from the car dealership he owned. I remember once driving my buddies to the Bee Hive after polishing off a bottle. When I pulled into the parking lot, I ran into a pole and shattered the front end and my windshield. My buddies jumped out of the car and scattered. That was the first of six cars I wrecked in high school. Dad would always get me another car from his dealership—no accountability for the spoiled. Nothing changed. I kept drinking and entertaining, loving the way alcohol made me feel.

What was going on beneath the surface? I had ADD—*Attention Deficit Disorder*. I was desperate—*desperate*—for attention and affection. My brother was better looking and a better athlete. I tried to fit in at school but to no avail. I tried out for the basketball team five times but was cut each time. I never made the football team. I tried out for the baseball team but didn't make it. I struggled in the classroom. This is when I started comparing myself to others.

Maybe it was because I thought I was an accident. At that stage of my parents' lives, it's not that I wasn't loved—but I was kind of an inconvenience. They were socialites. Mom, a model, and Dad, a dealership owner, would go out every Friday and Saturday night. On weekdays, I remember Dad often going to the bar at lunch with his dealership buddies, coming home to take a nap, then having three or four more martinis at home. My parents didn't really hold me accountable, which might explain why I always got a new car whenever I wrecked one. They loved me, just differently.

Mom was more present than my father—never once missing one of my swim meets—but it's apparent to me now that my parents' prime concern was being perceived as successful, as an ideal reflection of the American Dream. They cared a lot about the carefully crafted facade on the outside. I say this respectfully, but Mom fulfilled the model stereotype. She reminded me of Joan Crawford—refined, beautiful, appearing as if she always "had it together." Self-conscious in high school about my large nose, Mom once said to me, "Well, let's just get that taken care of." My parents were professionals at putting perfume on the pig. In other words, making a situation look better than it is with some kind of outward appearance. Putting perfume on a stinky old pig makes us think it smells better…but does it?

I followed the same path. I recklessly chased attention and affection at all costs. I was determined to be someone other than myself. Once in high school I remember a girl who I was interested in coming over to my house. I pointed at a picture of my brother and told her it was me. He was five years older and much better looking. She had to have thought I was insane. Delusion and fantasy disguised my pain. Alcohol only intensified my fantasies.

You might have a different journey, but aren't we all chasing attention and affection on some level? Don't we all try to fill the voids our wounds left? Don't we all from time to time get too caught up in putting perfume on the pig instead of journeying deeper into our own souls? It's in our own striving for attention—our attention deficit disorder—that some kind of addiction often creeps in.

The first step of Celebrate Recovery, a Christian-based recovery program, says, "We **ADMITTED** we were powerless over our addictions and compulsive behaviors—that our lives had become unmanageable." What is it in our lives that we need to admit? Admitting brings freedom, and the reason it brings freedom—and *power*—is because of the humility we let in when we admit.

In our own insecurity, we fear admitting we are powerless. Our insecurities are usually what we try to mask the most. Insecure about my looks, I ridiculously pointed toward that picture of my brother. We never talked about Dad having a drinking problem, though we all knew he did. After I wrecked my third or fourth car, I remember Mom telling me, "Don't tell your grandparents." Exposing my problems would have cracked the facade of the "All-American Family" in the suburbs with a big house and several cars in the driveway.

The truth is that most people go their whole lives masking their insecurities. I love my parents, but it's probably fair to say that they weren't very introspective during my childhood and adolescent years. Had it not been for drugs and alcohol, which pushed me to the edge of a cliff in which I had no choice but question the path that took me there, perhaps I would've gone my whole life masking my insecurities, too. Masking our insecurities is natural and human. It takes a lot of inner work to confront the deeply-embedded pain within our hearts and minds, the voids within our very being.

Masking might be the most popular form of dealing with pain in this country. Marketing campaigns cater to our own insecurities and dare us to buy their products to fill the void within ourselves. This is why many of them are so effective. They connect with us on a level so deep that most of us do not even understand, catering to our subconscious and our wounds. They are manipulative, seeking to exploit the most vulnerable aspects within ourselves. We wear masks so that we don't have to deal with reality. On social media, the exact same dynamic is on display. Have you ever seen somebody on social media unveil the messiness of their life? Probably not often. We usually share the steak after it's cooked, not when the cow is being cut up. People tend to share their idealized image of themselves with their followers, fueling everyone else's fantasies.

To *admit* powerlessness, or anything in our lives for that a matter, we all must be ruthlessly honest about our lives. Honesty is for everyone who wants to transform themselves and become a better human. I love the term "self-honesty." I recently heard someone pose the question: *How do we gain confidence?* The answer: doing what we promised ourselves we would do by sticking to our values. Frankly, a lot of people don't know what values are. Values are what you value. So, how do we lose our confidence? By *not* doing what we want to do. By not doing what we value. When we do what we say we're going to do, we are building self integrity. If we don't have self-integrity, we won't have integrity with anyone else.

For twenty-eight years, I had a vain mentality. Life began and ended with me. I was narcissistic, egotistical, pleasure-seeking, and determined to look good. It's fair to say my life revolved around the question, "How do I look?" I never walked by a mirror I didn't notice. Many people's lives, I'd argue, revolve around that same question. Maybe you care more about your job title than the attractiveness of the person staring back at you in the mirror, but it's appearance-centered nonetheless. On my journey, I was often slapped in the face with the reality that my life did not look good. In high school, I wanted to be an athlete; I wasn't. I wanted to be popular; I wasn't. I wanted to be attractive; but all I saw in the mirror was my large nose and floppy ear. Alcohol and drugs were my fuel for fantasizing and numbing a pain that I was too unaware to know existed—a trend that would continue for the next decade.

If Step 1 is rooted in honesty, then the opposite of Step 1 is denial. Denial is *not* a river in Egypt (i.e. the Nile). My life spun around denial.

But I've come to believe that life is too short to *not* be honest with ourselves and others. As this book begins, I invite you to anchor yourself in relentless honesty. What do you need to admit? In what area of your life do you feel powerless? What within yourself has become unmanageable? Consider this definition of addiction from our friend, Webster: "a strong inclination to do, use, or indulge in something repeatedly." So the question is: Do you feel addicted to something? Taking that deeper, what's your *heart's* addiction? Your habits, your heart's hangups?

In 1 Samuel 16:7, we read that the Lord says to Samuel, "The Lord does not look at the things people look at. People look at the outward appearance, but the Lord looks at the heart." 1 Peter 3:3-4 echoes this notion, "Your beauty should not come from outward adornment, such as elaborate hairstyles and the wearing of gold jewelry or fine clothes. Rather, it should be that of your inner self, the unfading beauty of a gentle and quiet spirit, which is of great worth in God's sight." No matter what you believe, that's a good path to walk down.

For me, my Christian faith has animated my own inward journey, but you don't have to be a Christian to ask yourself introspective questions; to get curious about the deeper issues in your own life; to evaluate that which resides in your heart. As the apostle Paul once wrote, "I do not understand what I do. For what I want to do I do not do, but what I hate I do." The honest *admitting* that the first step entails invites us to look at our lives through a different lens beyond the facade we've constructed and our own self-focused motives. The heart is where change begins.

What is it you would like to change?

If you and I really want to grow, this question must be answered on the soul level, not the worldly level. For example, "I want to make more money," or "I'd like to find a house with a basement," are not good answers to that question. The 12 Steps and Celebrate Recovery invite us into a journey that transforms us into more loving, selfless humans. Our answer to the question *must* guide us inward rather than further into the myths related to our own facades. We should confront the perfume-on-the-pig narrative. This brings an honest answer to the surface. Maybe it's something that is difficult to say out loud. Maybe it's something that makes you blush. My guess is that it's something you'd prefer that people not know, even the closest people in your life, perhaps *especially* the closest people in your life. We can't let the embarrassment that rises up become shame. In other words, don't let mistakes *in* our lives make us believe that we *are* a mistake. Guilt can be constructive when we ask ourselves, "What can I learn from this?" Shame is debilitating.

In John Maxwell's *The 15 Invaluable Laws of Growth*, he says that "you must know yourself to grow yourself." This echoes Socrates' famous, "Know thyself." Growth, he says, is not a natural process in most people's lives. It is easier to remain stagnant; to become reactive when life presses in on our wounds; to never ask oneself the hard questions and refrain from confronting difficult truths. There's a reason why they're called "growing pains."

Growth *is* painful. Getting honest with ourselves and evaluating what is happening beneath the surface of our lives will likely reveal some painful realities. *Admitting* powerlessness requires so much humility. And humility is where we get *freedom*. If you are used to feeling like you are in control—always "calling the shots" in life—this introductory step might feel as if you are being emptied. There are few things more humbling and scary in life than surrender…*admission*…humility.

But what is more painful than growth is venturing through life reacting to the darkness we carry. Unwilling for so long to bring the truth to the surface, I hurt my kids, my wife, my employees, my friends, and, through it all, myself. Refusing to name what we'd like to change hurts ourselves because our pride prevents us from becoming who God made us to be or tapping into our full potential as a leader—as a human.

If you are hesitant to take this next step, assess your resistance. In other words, where is the resistance coming from? Maybe it's the past, fear of the future, an insecurity, or shame. In Maxwell's book, there are eight gaps in learning that Maxwell names. They are worth spending some time with, as these gaps will look differently depending on your own unique personality and story.

The first gap is the Assumption Gap, which is assuming we will automatically grow. The truth is that we don't automatically do anything as it relates to transformation until we make a decision. Where in your life do you assume something is going to change but it never does? Get specific. Be intentional.

The second gap is the Knowledge Gap, which is not knowing how to grow. Knowledge is a billion-dollar-a-day business. Just go to YouTube or scroll through podcasts. Self-knowledge, however, is all together different. It requires introspection and honesty about one's circumstance.

The third gap is the Timing Gap, which is deciding it's not the right time to grow. I'm in my sixties, and I have to give you a little bit of advice I wish I would have adapted years ago: don't waste time; *now* is the time. There is never a better time to grow than now.

The fourth gap is the Mistake Gap, which is being paralyzed by the fear of making mistakes on our growth journeys. Don't be paralyzed by mistakes. I used to be so afraid of mistakes because of how I thought they made me look. Now I *love* mistakes. Mistakes are how we get to the next level in our transformation as we ask the question, "What did I learn?" Mistakes have become my greatest teachers.

The fifth is the Perfection Gap, which is having to find the best path forward before embarking upon it. We are never going to be perfect. Let's get over ourselves. The second we think we've found the perfect path is when we encounter yet another dead end. We may as well start journeying. It's in the journeying through unknown spaces that our transformation unfolds.

Sixth is the Inspiration Gap, which is not feeling like starting. Tony Robbins says that there is no such thing as laziness, just impotent goals. In other words, if our goals aren't good enough (or if they're too easy), then we need to find ones that move us toward our purpose. We need to ask ourselves what it is we really want and why we want it (we'll talk about this later). What is it that gets you out of bed in the morning?

Seventh is the Comparison Gap, which is feeling like others are better, thus finding it pointless to try to better oneself. Welcome to the world of social media. Many are paralyzed in their lives because they spend too much time comparing themselves to others on Facebook and Instagram. It's the work of darkness in our world that baits us into comparing ourselves to others. God has blessed you with *this* life. Each of us is "fearfully and wonderfully made" (Psalm 139:14), created "to do good works, which God prepared in advance for us to do" (Ephesians 2:10). Comparison is a very dangerous place. In recovery we learn to accept that God loves us and that we are uniquely made.

Lastly is the Expectation Gap, which is mistakenly thinking the road would be easier than it is. In AA they say to be careful of your expectations. I disagree. I love high expectations, but only high expectations that come with self-love and acceptance.

If you are having a hard time answering the question, "What would you like to Change?" take a look at these gaps. What are the gaps in your transformation? Those gaps are actually portals to change.

I'm not proud of a lot of things in my life, but one of the things I'm most proud of is my relationship with my kids. Even when we didn't always see eye-to-eye, I made sure I was always there for them physically and emotionally. They saw me make plenty of mistakes as a recovering person, but I hope I modeled for them, in some way, what it was like to go inward and invite introspection. Putting perfume on the pig will perhaps always be a temptation of mine—the lies we tell ourselves are sometimes hard to break—but over time I believe I have exposed the myth for what it was and is. I can still hear my mother say to me, "We can take care of that," as I was embarrassed by my big nose in high school. This came from the best place she knew as a mother based on what was modeled for her by her parents. As I saw insecurities rise up in the lives of my children, I tried to have a different narrative. That was and always is, "You're beautiful just the way you are." And, by the way, so are you.

I invite you to say this to yourself as you begin this journey. It might be tempting to beat yourself up (been there, done that) as you bring to the surface what you have always feared confronting. Shame might try to seize your heart. As I sponsor addicts through Celebrate Recovery and coach individuals in business and life, shame is single-handedly the force that sends my peeps (sponsees, clients) spiraling back into their addiction or self-defeating behavior. It is the ultimate gap in learning that prevents them from moving forward. Just as I defined myself by my looks in high school and later on in life by the mistakes I made under the influence of alcohol and cocaine, my peeps too struggle to get past this barrier of defining themselves by their flaws.

Yes, name what it is in your life that you want to change. Humbly *admit* a sense of powerlessness and that your life in this area has become unmanageable. And yet, let's not define ourselves by this darkness. Look into the mirror, with your big nose or floppy ear or dark past, with your hurts and habits and hangups, or whatever it may be, and remind yourself, "I am beautiful just the way I am."

There is a fascinating scene in John 5. Jesus, noticing a man who is "blind, lame, and paralyzed" near a pool, asks him, "Do you want to get well?" The question posed this chapter—*Do you want to change?*—reflects Jesus's question here. The man responds to Jesus that he has no one to help him bathe. Jesus responds, "Get up! Pick up your mat and walk." That is a command each of us must receive if we decide we want to get well. We must rise to our feet, pick up our mat, and move.

Your journey has brought you here, to the door of change, and there is no better place to be. Let me open the door for you.

Scan the QR code to watch a special message from Bart about Chapter One.

CHAPTER 2

TALE OF A CAR SALESMAN

I woke up to rumbling and screams downstairs. My vision was hazy, my mind foggy.

We had partied hard the night before, something that had become routine in my life and was spiraling out of control. It had begun with drinking alcohol in high school (with all those ridiculous performances at the Bee Hive) and escalated at college and in the years that followed. That was also when I discovered cocaine, weed, and acid. By the time I was in my late twenties, I was spending $4,000 or more a month on cocaine while working as a salesman at a car dealership in California. I was lost. My life was the west coast, car salesman version of *The Wolf of Wall Street* (not quite, but you get the point).

As I gathered my whereabouts and as my senses clicked back into place, I hurried downstairs to figure out what the commotion was. I couldn't drive home the night before, so I had stayed at a friend's house. The screams grew louder. I heard sirens approaching. There in the center of the living room, I saw Johnny—a party acquaintance from the night before—collapsed on the floor, foaming at the mouth. Apparently he had mixed heroine with cocaine, which was common in many overdoses back then. My friend Lonnie tried to give him mouth-to-mouth as I sat back and watched helplessly.

The next day at work, I was numb yet also unchanged. I did coke throughout the day. If I became anxious, I'd smoke weed to bring me back down. I drank and partied after work, seeking the next thrill.

There were so many wakeup calls in those days but nothing was enough to slow me from my reckless pleasure-seeking. My dad, my idol, died at fifty-nine years old from alcoholism, yet not even that could make me slow down to evaluate my own decision-making. There were evenings after partying when I drove home from San Jose to Santa Cruz on a two-lane mountain road and somehow made it home. One evening, high out of my mind, I swore I saw a horse in the road. Another time, barely functioning, I pulled over on the side of the road and fell asleep, only to be awakened by a cop hours later. Drinking and driving was unfortunately commonplace back then, but still it's shocking to consider how these "close calls" never ushered introspection. I was a narcissist who had built my life on chasing ego boosts—that desperate chase for attention and affection—and the thrill of it all made me think I was invincible. Alcohol and cocaine made me feel confident and "on top of the world."

I was a car salesman, and my life resembled the crude stereotype: perhaps well-put together on the outside with a house and a wife and a good car and a good job, but also manipulative, sleazy, and the exact opposite of honest. I was the center of my own universe, in a perpetual free-fall into selfishness. I was a pleasure-seeking zombie, determined always to get "mine." What would it take to wake me from my sleep?

The second step of Celebrate Recovery says that "We came to **BELIEVE** that a power greater than ourselves could restore us to sanity." You might sense a few strong verbs there: *came*, *believe*, and *restore*.

Everyone believes in something, but that something is usually way to shallow because it begins and ends with ourselves. Even staunch atheists still have faith in *something*. At that time in my life my world began and ended with selfish pleasure. But this "coming to believe" in a recovery sense entails having the *humility* to believe in something outside of ourselves, to have a deeper purpose beyond our own selfish ambitions. This *frees* us from the pressure of being the god of our own universes. Today I find my deeper purpose in Jesus Christ, but maybe for you your deeper purpose is love, service, or empowering others (which to me is what Jesus is all about). Each of us, in some way, must surrender to a source that is greater than ourselves.

Recovery is for everybody who believes in something better for their lives and has the humility to ask for help. The "Higher Power" discussed in AA could be as simple as touching a door knob and asking for help. The message is to stop believing the lie that everything is up to you and that you're the center of the universe. To experience the freedom of surrender. New-agers often talk about believing in something *within*, but what they mean by this is going inward toward something greater than themselves. Everybody is searching for something.

The person who doesn't believe in anything will fall for everything. That's exactly where I was in my party days. Any sign of attention, any nod of affection, anything that made me feel in control—that was what I followed. The child who was desperate for attention never evolved or grew up. I was an egotistical "Baby Bart" who was determined to get any and every pleasure I wanted. I never developed introspection or curiosity toward myself or, frankly, toward life. My trajectory in life was especially shallow, but all of us, on some level, are tempted to chase attention or affection or slip back into our childlike selfishness.

We all must believe in a power that is greater than ourselves, whatever that might mean to you. We are more than flesh and bone. Wayne Dyer said that we are spiritual beings having a human experience. We don't make our hearts pump. We don't control the millions of functions within our bodies that happen each minute. We don't make the world spin on its axis. We don't make it revolve around the sun. Whether or not you believe in God there is no denying that each of us are living, breathing miracles on this planet.

Maybe you, too, tend to believe the biggest lie in our culture that everything is up to you. Take a second and stop what you are doing. Slow your breathing. Place your hand on your heart. Feel its steady beat in the cup of your hand. Are you *really* in control? Are you *really* the center of the universe? Is everything *really* up to you? When you and I can stop and do this exercise, it can create a humility and a belief that there HAS to be something greater than ourselves.

In Matthew 22:36-40, we read about a scene between Jesus and the scribes where Jesus is asked which is the greatest commandment. Jesus replies, "Love the Lord your God with all your heart and with all your soul and with all your mind.' This is the first and greatest commandment. And the second is like it: 'Love your neighbor as yourself.'" In other words, get out of yourself. Christians often talk about "dying to self," which I believe means being "all in" with Jesus. Something that has nothing to do with yourself or your performance. Something that doesn't place *you* at the center. Whereas our culture and all our marketing campaigns usually fuel our selfish desires in some way, Jesus invites us to look outward with a loving gaze: toward God and toward others.

Came. Believe. Restore. The victory is that as we believe in a power that is greater than ourselves, as we leave behind our selfish ways, *we* are the ones who are restored.

❖❖❖

What do you believe in?

Seriously, think about it. Even if you aren't spiritually inclined, you believe in love, right? How about the value of relationships? Or the importance of taking care of your loved ones? Or being there for your friends when they're going through a tough time? Or making this community or world a better place?

All of these things, you might notice, are outward-focused. Even if you're a dreamer or a workaholic or an entrepreneur with lofty goals, my guess would be that if you took a step back from your pursuits, if you got *really* honest with yourself, what you'd find most important would be the *people* around you. Your kids. Your spouse. Your family members. Your friends. The people you're leading.

Last chapter we asked ourselves the question, *What is it that you would like to change?* Well, naming what you believe in might be one of your routes to change, to restoration, to peace that we all crave. During my days of debauchery, I never dared to ask myself, *What do I believe in?* I neglected soul. I neglected depth. I lived on the very surface of my life for years, never tapping into my potential as a human with a spirit and soul, with a heart and a mind.

Zoom out. Look at your life as a whole. On cemetery headstones, it shows the date someone was born and the date they die. What does your dash look like? It's in the dash when we define our lives. Consider your life as the blip that it is. Think about the day you'll leave this earth and pass from this life into the next. What is it that you want people to say about you? What is your legacy? What would you want your life to be about? Your answer is what you believe in.

In John Maxwell's *The 15 Invaluable Laws of Growth*, he says that "growth stops when you lose the tension between where you are and where you could be." In other words, when you get comfortable, growth stops. My greatest victories in life have come when I've been willing to get *uncomfortable.*

Uncovering what you believe in will point you toward who you can be. If you believe in God, then you will strive to become a more loving person through prayer, scripture reading, and learning more about faith. If you believe in love, you'll aim to care for and serve the most important people in your life. If you believe in justice, you'll seek to come alongside the forgotten and broken. Belief, at its best, leads to restoration not only within ourselves, but those around us benefit as a result.

Many will refrain from ever naming what they believe in because the tension between where they are and where they could be is too uncomfortable to bear (as it was for me). But the tension points us toward how we need to change. Yes, it's *hard* to change. As Tony Robbins says, people will do anything to avoid pain and anything to gain pleasure. It's tempting to think it's easier to go through life being selfish and reactive—to never grow—but this is actually more difficult because of the pain and destruction it causes. Never inviting the tension of change makes it impossible to find peace and restoration. As Maxwell once wrote, "God's gift to us is potential and our gift to Him is developing it." It doesn't always feel good but it's a necessary part of transformation.

The key to all this is that short-term pain—working the steps—equals long-term gain. And short-term gain (pleasure) equals long-term pain. One thing I do now that is really powerful for me is getting clear about what I value. I get up every morning at around four thirty. I write down my beliefs, my values. That starts with God at the top, then my recovery and health, then my wife, then my kids. Then, in no particular order, I write down personal development, career, finances, relationships, and leisure. This list makes up my ten values.

Then I rate myself on how I'm doing with each of those. That exercise really got me focused on a daily basis. Everything we do is about one day at a time. Everything. The purpose of spending 5-15 minutes on this exercise is that it gives me clarity one day at a time. Whether you're an addict or not, you're reading this book for a purpose, and none of this happens if we don't take it one day at a time. "One day at a time" is a huge part of recovery. Victory doesn't happen without one day at a time.

Let's take an honest look at our lives. Let's get direct. Let's consider the different wakeup calls our lives might be revealing to us. Let's open ourselves up to changing the unhealthy patterns that prevent us from awakening to our full spiritual potential, or, as Jesus said, living life to the fullest. Let's open ourselves to the tension of change and the power of belief.

Scan the QR code to watch a special message from Bart about Chapter Two.

CHAPTER 3

LOOSENING THE TIE

I thought I was at work alone. I finished a beer from the twelve-pack under my desk, then slipped into the bathroom at the dealership to do a line of cocaine, gearing up for another night of partying. Moments later my manager had snuck up behind me in the bathroom. We made eye-contact. He pointed beneath his nose, motioning to me to clean myself up, making it clear that he knew what I had been doing.

"Damn, those sugar donuts are *awesome*," I joked.

He wasn't having it. I'd been caught red-handed.

The next day, I called in sick. The day after that, I returned to work. My boss was in my office waiting for me first thing that morning. I could've expected that.

"We need to chat," he said.

At that point in my life I was beginning to realize something was wrong. Maybe my daughter being born had something to do with it, I don't know, but I was beginning to realize that my addiction to attention and affection was bringing more pain than peace, though I certainly didn't have those words for that then. My heart was still hardened and I still was not introspective in the slightest, but I was beginning to realize just how miserable I was. My raging alcoholism and drug addiction was making me more irritable and angry at work and at home. I was narcissistic, striving for attention from the opposite sex (all my friends were women), spending over half of my monthly paycheck on cocaine, and led a life that was built around partying and chasing the next thrill. I was broken. I was lost. I was miserable.

"Listen," my boss said, "I know you've been drinking at work. I know you've been doing cocaine at work. I'm going to have to let you go."

"Why?" I asked, like an idiot, as if those two reasons weren't enough. I think my brain was just trying to fight it. My life was so wrapped up in image and success.

"C'mon, Bart," he said bluntly, "you've left me with no choice."

I paused, "If I get some help, can I come back?"

"Of course," said my boss.

He left my office, and that was that.

I unbuttoned my top button, loosened my tie, and may have let out an audible, "Phew." Much to my surprise, I was overwhelmed with a sense of *relief*. Not anger. Not rejection. Not disappointment. *Relief*.

That's because, for perhaps the first time in my life, some sense of conviction had been stirring within me, though I certainly didn't have the maturity to act upon it. Months before I had seen a former co-worker of mine, Bob, who I used to party with all the time. I was shocked by his appearance. He looked incredible! He seemed healthy, strong, fit, and even had a certain glimmer in his eyes, a kind of ground-edness in his demeanor I hadn't seen before. "You look great!" I told him. "What's your secret?"

"I got sober," he told me.

I was taken aback. "How in the world did you do that?" I laughed, thinking of what-had-to-have-been the hundreds of beers and lines we did together. But I was intrigued. Leave it to me, the person who was sure to look into any mirror he passed, to first consider sobriety because of someone's appearance. Cocaine and alcohol had left me skinny and sickly, and I knew it.

"I went to rehab at the Adrian Center in Santa Cruz," he told me. "Do you want their number?"

Wanting to look like my friend, just as I had wanted to look like my brother all those years, I gave the Adrian Center a call. A meeting was eventually arranged between me and a woman named Reba. "We can get you in right now for thirty days," she said.

"I can't do thirty days," I laughed. I was the *finance director* at a deal-ership! I was important! How could I take thirty days off work to "get clean"? And why was getting sober so important anyway? I just wanted to look different.

But then one day ran into another. I remember once partying hard midday on a weekday and thinking to myself, "Why?" At work the next day I remember it dawning on me that I had never sold a car sober before.

I was beginning to realize that my life was becoming unmanageable.

That's perhaps why I experienced immense *relief* when my boss fired me. Now I had the time to hopefully heal.

I left work, got a ride down to the bar, drank a few beers, then went home and drank a few more as I sat out in the sun. I thought to myself, "You know what? It's time."

The next morning, I woke up crying like a newborn. I was desperate, not because I lost my job, but because I was so ashamed of my addiction. I got on my knees and again loosened my proverbial tie. I asked God for help. In that moment I got the intuition to call the Adrian Center.

Within two hours, I had checked myself in.

The third step of Celebrate Recovery says that, "We **MADE A DECISION** to turn our lives and our wills over to the care of God." Again, sense the strength of the verb in this step: *made a decision*. This step propels us into fully confronting our addiction; to taking the necessary *next* step in whatever it is we'd like to change. Rather than flippantly venturing through life mindlessly reacting to every potential promise of attention or affection, this step brings us a certain clarity. Our lives have become unmanageable, and, though we may not know our futures, we know *exactly* what decision we have to make in order to move toward health and integration.

Consider your addiction. Take a look at your attachments. Contemplate the thing in your life you would most like to change. What's the decision you *know* you have to make? That thing that has been pressing on your heart for a while now? That nagging notion your conscience keeps bringing to the surface?

In the New Testament there's a theme known as *metanoia*, a word that is somewhat difficult to translate from Greek to English, but means something similar to "a change of mind" or "repentance" or "conversion." The word "pivot" has certainly become something of a cliche as its been overblown in leadership circles, but pivoting is precisely the notion behind *metanoia*. You're heading in one direction, but then love or transformation stirs you to go an entirely *different* direction. This is essential to authentic conversion.

You might recall the famous New Testament story about Paul as he was journeying to Damascus. Paul was a pharisee who was committed to persecuting Christians and putting a stop to this new Christian religion that was invigorating the hearts and minds of many. He did not know that he was living a life of sin, but he was. Maybe he, too, was chasing attention and affection through the realm of religious zeal.

As he journeyed, however, we read in the book of Acts that he was blinded by a radiant light which made him fall to the ground. Jesus Christ, the Risen Savior, then says to him (Acts 9:4), "Saul (who would later be known as Paul), why do you persecute me?" This confrontation was the beginning of Paul's conversion. For the next three days we read that Paul "was blind, and did not eat or drink anything." This is the start of the terrifying "unknowing" that we all experience after we make a decision or pivot and commit fully to this new direction.

As you make a decision, prepare your mind for this unknowing. I had no idea what the Adrian Center would entail. I did not have an introspective bone in my body. I had never been to counseling. I had always followed what "felt good" at all costs. But God does not ask us to have it all figured out. God simply asks us to respond to the call—the blinding light that meets us on the road in the form of our heart's conviction or our conscience—and partner with transformation.

Maybe you're not an addict, but it still might be time for you to get curious about your life. I see that as my civic responsibility: to come alongside people so that they don't have to experience the same brokenness I felt. The sooner we learn the steps, the sooner we get on the road to recovery.

What's pulling on your heartstrings? What's the light that keeps invading your reality? What conviction keeps seizing you? Make a decision in response to that light. Trust your new direction, though you might not know where this unfamiliar path will take you. With this decision, with this change of direction, our journey of transformation has officially begun.

❖❖❖

One of the great leadership books of all time is Og Mandino's *The Greatest Salesman in the World*, which tells the story of a poor camel boy, Hafid, whose transformation leads to success and abundance. It's Hafid's discovery of The Ten Scrolls—each scroll containing wisdom that is simple, practical, and profound—that propels him forward on his journey. To this day, I read through The Ten Scrolls just about every week. Each scroll has a way of anchoring me in truth when it is so easy to become distracted.

The "Scroll Marked I" is titled, "Today I begin a new life," and starts with these words: "Today I begin a new life. Today I shed my old skin, which hath, too long, suffered the bruises of failure and the wounds of mediocrity. Today I am born anew and my birthplace is a vineyard where there is fruit for all."

Each of us gets to decide whether we begin anew. The "bruises of failure and the wounds of mediocrity" might try to make us feel ashamed or worthless or far too comfortable. But when we get that internal nudge to change, we can make a decision that says, "Nah, forget it," or make one that says, "Yep, let's try something new."

Our decisions determine our destiny. We all know the definition of insanity—doing the same thing over and over again and expecting to get different results—but let's consider insanity in the context of decisions. If we never choose change, then we're going insane. That's because *everyone* has something they need to change. As human beings we are literally born *into* change. We grow. We develop. We learn. Everything around us changes as well. The seasons, the earth, people, plants, and animals—the only constant in all of creation is *change*. To fight or ignore this reality is to go against nature itself.

Patrick Lencioni, a great leadership mentor and author of *The Five Dysfunctions of a Team* (which are the "absence of trust, fear of conflict, lack of commitment, avoidance of accountability, and attention to results"), once shared on his podcast about an intervention he did with a former client. When his client, who was a CEO, gathered feedback from his executive team through a questionnaire that evaluated his leadership style, he eventually threw his hands up in the air and said, "It says here that I'm not very patient! Who said that?" Of course no one raised their hand. "C'mon, tell me!" he exclaimed.

The irony here is palpable. One of the many things we sense in this story is a total inability by the CEO to begin anew. Instead of these evaluations igniting his curiosity, he becomes protective of his ego. Instead of his revealed blindspots and shortcomings leading to growth, he feels threatened. In being confronted with the truth, he hunkers down into a comfortable lie. Can you relate to any of this? This is a natural, human reaction whenever something chips away at our ego, but we must evaluate it nonetheless.

Each of us, every day, must choose to *loosen the tie*: to let go a little, to surrender a bit more, to adopt a posture of humility and be unafraid to ask for help. It can be scary to loosen the tie. It's nice to feel like we have it all together, to project out to the world the idealized image of ourselves. This is social media, right? We post how we *want* to be perceived—usually as successful, happy, or sexy—and then we receive positive feedback based on this curated, airbrushed image. Sadly, this is sometimes the church as well: people walking into the sanctuary dressed in their Sunday best, trying to come across as perfectly polished to people in their community. The reality, however, is that church has always consisted of sinners who gather together to lift up one another in their brokenness and receive God's grace. Loosening the tie requires engaging the messiness of life—the stuff that isn't fun to talk about, the stuff that contradicts the polished image we project—so that true transformation can happen; so that we can *truly* begin to grow.

I once had a boss at a dealership in my twenties who resembled everything I wanted to become. He was charismatic, slick, and successful. He owned multiple businesses, several houses, and had girlfriends all around him. I wanted to be like him because he seemed to get anything that he wanted. His success, in my mind, positioned him to never have to say "no" to anything. But when he was in his thirties, everything came crashing down. His wife caught him in an affair. His businesses got audited. He ended up losing *everything*. He never loosened the tie.

It might feel scary, but I promise there is something freeing about loosening the tie. Why do we so often think that we have to come across as having it all together? We know that *no one* has it all together; that no one has it figured out; that everyone is on a journey and carries burdens that no one can see. In loosening the tie, our idols lose their grip on us. We become less controlled by our surface-level gods that drain us of our energy and peace. We experience the *relief* of knowing that all is not up to us.

Every morning, I get on my knees and pray the Alcoholics Anonymous prayer from Step 3: "God, I offer myself to Thee — to build with me and to do with me as Thou wilt. Relieve me of the bondage of self, that I may better do Thy will. Take away my difficulties, that victory over them may bear witness to those I would help of Thy Power, Thy Love, and Thy Way of life. May I do Thy will always!"

Getting on my knees to pray and bowing my head is a daily confession that I cannot tackle my day alone—they are all symbols of surrender. This movement positions my heart to be humble when my tendency is to slip into selfishness. It positions my mind to be open when my tendency is to think it's all up to me. It positions my soul to abide in God rather than letting my ego call all the shots.

Together, let's loosen our ties and experience relief from the bondage of ourselves. Let's surrender to a deeper purpose beyond our own selfish desires.

Scan the QR code to watch a special message from Bart about Chapter Three.

CHAPTER 4

THE ROOT AND
THE REASON

I sought help through the Adrian Center because I thought I had a cocaine problem, not an alcohol problem, as crazy as that might sound. It didn't matter that I wrecked six cars in high school or that I was drinking a six-pack of beer (at least) a day or that every time I drank it was to get drunk. My skinniness was connected to cocaine. The inside of my nose being fried was connected to cocaine. I thought the Adrian Center would help me solve my cocaine addiction and then I could go on living and, yes, probably partying the way I had before.

But as I was introduced to the 12 Steps at the Adrian Center, removed from my toxic lifestyle patterns, I began to see that my problems extended beyond cocaine. I still couldn't say the word "humility." I still struggled to see my own character flaws and lapses in integrity. But within merely a week at the Adrian Center, I was surprised by the level of realization that was beginning to settle within me: *I was an alcoholic too.* Later on in the program other issues revealed themselves as well, like anger, control, seeking attention from women, and co-dependency.

After a couple weeks in the program, I had a review meeting with my counselor, Gus, a six-foot-four, rough-around-the-edges kind of guy. "You're not going to stay sober," he told me bluntly.

"What do you mean?" I asked, taken aback, thinking that sponsors in recovery should be more positive and empowering.

"You still have your kid, your house, and your cars," Gus said. "Your bottom is way too high. You'll never make it until you hit rock-bottom."

I wanted to punch him in the face, but it may have been strategic on his part. Maybe he sensed my arrogance and my massive blindspots. Maybe he was trying to push me to see other patterns in my life that might help me reach rock-bottom internally so I wouldn't have to lose more externally. Whatever the case, he lit my drive and ambition.

Realizing that I was also an alcoholic was a breakthrough for me. I may not have been very introspective or spiritually curious yet, but this realization outlined a path that would continue the remainder of my life: when you *truly* make a decision to change (Step 3), you unlock more doors to transformation that you didn't know existed. I thought the Steps would help me simply cut out cocaine, but they were already leading me to a *complete* 180-degree change of direction: the conviction to undergo a total transformation in my lifestyle and, ultimately, my very self.

Change is like that. It expands. This might sound crazy or scary, but it's actually freeing. It's like hiking up a mountain. The farther you venture up the trail, it might become more challenging and strenuous; but the horizon also expands; the views become more beautiful; awe and wonder stir your heart.

This is the potential and excitement in soul-searching. If we never go on the journey of transformation, then our decision to never change will inevitably lead us to a rock-bottom moment where we'll be forced to change anyway. For many addicts, this rock-bottom often ends up being prison or bankruptcy or isolation as those we love push us out of their lives. I got lucky that none of these happened to me when they very well could have.

I think that's what Gus was trying to tell me when he said I hadn't lost enough to change. To *keep* the change, you truly have to *hate* how you've been living. If you don't hate it, then you likely won't do enough to fix it. But if the pain is deep enough, you'll do *anything* you can to fix it. If we're struggling to change, could it be because we don't hate our darkness enough to fully confront it? Taking a moral inventory helps us to develop a hatred for the darkness because we see more clearly the negative effects our addictions or attachments are having on ourselves and those we love.

If we don't want to experience the pain and humiliation of rock-bottom externally (in our careers, relationships, etc.) then we have to get there internally and begin the climb. The journey might become rocky and at times feel impossible, but the tradeoff is that in transformation you'll experience more beauty—and *peace!*—than ever before.

The fourth step of Celebrate Recovery invites us to make a "searching and fearless moral inventory of ourselves." In my opinion, our continual process of transformation always goes back to this step. This soul-searching is a deep dive into our hearts, minds, personalities, blindspots, and tendencies. It helps us discover the root and the reason behind our actions—the *why* beneath our addictions or attachments. For example, what's happening emotionally within ourselves when we do drugs or get drunk or escape into pornography? Sadness? Anger? Stress? Getting curious about what is happening beneath the surface will help us to diagnose the deeper problem rather than mask the symptom. What in our past might be contributing to the resistance we experience in changing? What are some blindspots or tendencies we might have in each of our unique personalities that fuel our attachments?

I learned at the Adrian Center that my addiction to cocaine was more emotional than it was physical. Cocaine gave me a euphoric high that made me feel bulletproof. I'd slip into the bathroom on a plane, do a line, and walk out feeling like I was "the man," a real badass who could do anything. Thus the goal in recovery was not only to quit doing cocaine but to change the *thoughts*—there's that word again—I had about cocaine. To believe that I was competent and personable enough to live life, even if I was sober. To one day trust that God's love alone was enough to make me feel full and whole and confident. To realize that I already possessed everything I needed to be successful *without* using cocaine. As the Apostle Paul (also known as Saul) wrote in Ephesians 1:3, "Praise be to the God and Father of our Lord Jesus Christ, who has blessed us in the heavenly realms with *every spiritual blessing* (emphasis mine) in Christ." To realize that we already possess every spiritual blessing within our very beings frees us to not have to cling to anything else for attention or affection.

The failure to diagnose the root and reason beneath our addictions and attachments is why, I think, people often struggle to leave their addictions behind. They're too focused on "not doing that thing" but there's actually something deeper that's making them want to do that thing. It's not just the behavior, it's the root. Maybe we flee to our addictions (the symptom) whenever someone makes us feel the same way our parents made us feel. Or whenever the lie we've always told ourselves resurfaces. Or whenever we seek to fill the void a loved one left. Exploring these underlying issues will help us to gain a deeper understanding for ourselves and why our addictions have a hold on us.

I must say, however, that this step *must* be met with curiosity and empathy for ourselves. This step can be intense. It might require a deep dive into our childhoods or backgrounds or sinful actions. To get to the root, you have to do some digging. Reliving some of the most destructive moments in your life can be painful, and, again, self-contempt or shame may tempt us to believe their lies.

Sponsorship, remember, is somebody walking right alongside you. A good sponsor knows the steps, has life lessons to share, and has been in recovery for a long time. My first sponsor is eighty five and is in a nursing home in Oregon. I still keep in touch with him today. At the beginning of my recovery journey, I talked to him every day, and we met every week. As we worked through the steps, my sponsor took me through an inventory worksheet. Celebrate Recovery has an inventory worksheet as well with five columns. I hope you find this helpful:

- **The Person:** Who is the object of my resentment or fear?
- **The Cause:** What specific action did that person take that hurt me?
- **The Effect:** What effect did that action have on my life?
- **The Damage:** What damage did that action do to my basic security, social instincts, or sexual instincts?
- **My Part:** What part of the resentment am I responsible for? Who are the people I have hurt? How have I hurt them?

Keep in mind why I'm telling you this: there is victory on the other side. We can finally live a life of peace and abundance when the darkness is in the rearview mirror. But you have to pick up the mat first. Keep your eyes on the promise of victory and peace. If we're in motion, we don't have to live in the rearview mirror anymore. We don't have to live a life of regret. We get to live a life of victory. You can't do this alone. The whole magic of AA is broken people helping others.

Several years ago, I was working through the steps with a CR group because I still didn't like who I was. I wasn't drinking or doing drugs, but I had replaced those addictions with different behaviors. As many addicts will tell you, "flipping addictions" is not uncommon. That's why it's important to continually work the steps. This, however, was a *very* deep dive into the Steps—one step per month in a group therapy format—the goal being to discover things we were yet to uncover within ourselves and within our stories. It was intensive and, in retrospect, I probably should have sought out more professional guidance to help me navigate the intensity. As I shared with the group my story and dove into the specifics of my shortcomings, it was so painful to become reacquainted with the ugliness of who I used to be. I began to feel a very real sense of shame and despair.

That entire month as we worked through the fourth step, I guess you could say that I caved to self-contempt. I doubted the truths about who God said that I was—all the spiritual truths I had learned over the decades. The Bible says that we are loved and adored, but I slipped into believing that I was messed up and beyond repair. I became defined by my sins and the mistakes that hurt those who I loved the most. Reliving the darkest parts of my story in such an intense way—being so absorbed in my past wrongdoings—almost made me feel like I had never changed or gotten sober. I began focusing more on my ugliest moments rather than the many victories God had brought me through over the decades. As a consequence, I had a relapse. Not with drugs or alcohol, thank goodness, but with addictive tendencies in a different area of my life. How has the human search for attention and affection become warped in your own life?

A "searching and fearless moral inventory of ourselves" leaves no stone unturned. It avoids no questions. It explores *anything* that might contribute to our struggle with our addiction or attachment. But the step cannot be attempted without grace or radical self-compassion. Surround yourself with a team that loves you enough to be honest with you—with a counselor and/or sponsor and accountability partners. As you read you'll notice that this step will be woven throughout the rest of the book. Consider making Psalm 139:23-24 your prayer: "Search me, God, and know my heart; test me and know my anxious thoughts. See if there is any offensive way in me, and lead me in the way everlasting."

Because self-awareness is so important to transformation, this is the step in which all others revolve around. Without "knowing thyself" (Socrates), we will venture through life reacting to our deepest pains and insecurities, always trying to fill the void.

❖❖❖

In Napoleon Hill's *Think and Grow Rich*, which I teach a course on, one of the dominant themes is that you are what you think about. In my case, all I thought about during my partying years was seeking attention and affection at all costs. My decisions reflected this. I was essentially an empty glass that could never be filled. Each thrill somehow left me feeling more empty than before. If we're going to evaluate what we think about, we have to consider our habits. Eighty percent of our behaviors are habits. At least fifty percent of those habits are usually bad habits. So how do you change yourself? You change your thinking, which is meant to replace your bad habits with good habits.

I teach a class called Self Image Mastery (created by my mentor, Paul Martinelli) that is based on Matthew Maltz's book, *Psycho-Cybernetics*. In the course, I like to guide students through a three-phase exercise. Feel free to go through each phase right now or adopt this exercise throughout your day.

Phase 1: Take a couple of minutes to pay attention to your thoughts.

Phase 2: Picture yourself in a theater watching each passing thought appear on the silver screen.

Phase 3: Notice the bad thoughts—those thoughts that don't serve you well—and actively replace them with a good thought.

For example, an unhealthy thought might sound like:

I am feeling a little anxious and insecure, I think I need to do a line to feel confident.

Which can be replaced with a more healthy thought:

It's natural and human for me to feel anxious and insecure, I need to take this time to pray or re-center myself and remember that my confidence comes from God or from within, not from any drug.

The key is to not only reframe the unhealthy thought with a healthy thought but follow up on the healthy thought with an *action*, which will help us to develop a good habit if this is practiced repeatedly.

Another related exercise that we learned in AA is to follow the unhealthy thought and see where it goes. This re-centers us by deconstructing the thought.

Mind: A drink would feel amazing right now.

Self: Okay, then what?

Mind: I'd probably have a few more.

Self: Okay, then what?
Mind: It would feel great.
Self: Okay, then what?
Mind: I'd probably have a few more.
Self: Okay, then what?
Mind: I would feel out of control and terrible.
Self: Okay, then what?
Mind: I would probably do the same thing the next day.
Self: Okay, then what?
Mind: My loved ones would know I was drinking again.
Self: Then what?
Mind: They would be really hurt.
Self: Then what?
Mind: I would have to work even harder to earn their respect back and get sober again. I may have to move out of the house. I may have to go back to treatment. I may have to go back to counseling. I would have to start all over.
Self: Okay, so is it worth it to order a drink?
Mind: No, I'm so proud that I've rebuilt trust with my loved ones and am going to keep working hard to make them happy and keep my heart, mind, and body healthy.

In the science of Neuro Linguistic Programming (NLP), practitioners of NLP talk about the power of anchoring positivity in order to change your habits. What are your first thoughts when you wake up in the morning? I admit that as I came to terms with all the horrible things I had done, I often awoke to thoughts that tried to tear me down and send me back to who I once was. It was as if the devil was in my mind, firing arrows of shame and negativity at my soul. Understanding NLP has helped me get more comfortable with looking in the mirror, puffing my chest out, and saying, "I *am* marvelous." I was once watching behind-the-scenes content from *The Voice*, and at one point Lionel Ritchie looked in the mirror, smiled, and said, "Oh my God, it's Lionel Ritchie." *That's* what we're talking about here. Replace the negative thinking with positive affirmations that you really believe—and do it with emotion.

If you've had little meditative or prayer practice, the idea of evaluating one's thoughts might sound impossible in the chaos of what you're dealing with. Maybe it sounds too intense. Start, instead, by taking a

DISC behavior assessment or another personality test. DISC stands for four personality types: Dominance, Influence, Steadiness, and Conscientiousness. These are good onramps for getting curious about your personality and inner world. In a DISC, you'll begin to discover your strengths, weaknesses, blindspots, and tendencies. *Nothing* that a DISC (or any other personality test for that matter) reveals is bad because your personality reflects how God uniquely designed you to be. The goal after taking a DISC is not to change your personality (that would be a real waste of time) but rather to become aware of the strengths you can lean into, as well as your own weaknesses in which you might need some accountability. A DISC might help you to see the origin of some of your unhealthy thoughts and to reframe them.

In my studies to become a DISC behavior assessment specialist, I learned about something called the Johari Window, which I implement with my companies and my teachings. The Johari Window was created by psychologists Joseph Luft and Harrington Ingham. It helps us to know ourselves so that we can uncover massive authenticity.

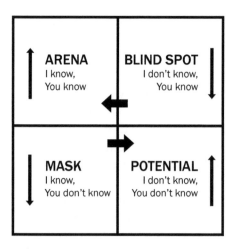

Picture a window with four panes. In the upper-left quadrant is your *arena*, which is information (attitude, behavior, feelings, talents) about oneself that is known by both yourself and others. Think about a close friend who knows you well.

To the right, in the upper-right quadrant, is your ***blindspot***—what others know about you but you are unaware of, like the fact that I was needy and desperate for attention. Think again about your close friend who knows something about you that you are yet to awaken to.

In the bottom-left quadrant is your *facade*, something that *you* know about yourself but no one else knows. This is also called a "mask," this thing I know about myself but don't let anyone in on it, not even a close friend. We all have masks, but for me personally I have often tried to mask the shame I carry from my past.

To the right, in the bottom-right quadrant, is your *potential* (which is unknown)—that which you nor anyone else knows about yourself, anything from unearthed skills to repressed trauma. As it's described in my training, potential is something that neither of us know yet.

The Johari Window provides a map for curious discovery. If we can increase our Arena, we can decrease our Blindspot. If we get rid of our Masks, guess what happens to our Potential? *It goes up.* The Arena and Potential quadrants expand as our Blindspot and Mask decrease. It might be worth asking some of your close friends some questions about your blindspots: *How can I become a better person or friend? What patterns in my life do you see that I don't?* It might also be worth asking yourself some questions about your facade: *In what ways do I fear being fully known? What are the insecurities I try to hide?* A good relationship with your sponsor and therapist really helps you to reveal some of these things. If you want to sign up for a DISC, email me at bart@bartnollenberger.com. I'll provide you with a discounted test and assessment.

It's impossible to be leaders if we aren't growing in self-awareness. The more we learn about ourselves, the more approachable and relatable we'll be. As a title of one of John Maxwell's books so perfectly says, everyone communicates but few connect. Before the Adrian Center I struggled to connect with people in a meaningful way because I knew nothing about myself. I was a drifter, floating from pleasure to pleasure, never really connecting with people heart-to-heart, not even in my committed relationships. As I began to know myself, my heart expanded, which helped me to have more compassion and curiosity for others.

Self-awareness might feel scary because it seems like we're bringing our weaknesses to the surface, but that's actually the fun of it once you get through the initial intensity of the darkness. Our weaknesses often become those places where we connect most with others. I'm a sponsor and a coach today because of my understanding of my own weaknesses. Without this understanding, my sponsees and clients wouldn't trust me.

I'm able to connect with them more deeply and serve them because they know they aren't alone in their own struggles.

We've gone over a lot in this chapter, and self-awareness will continue to remain a theme as this book unfolds, but I'll end on this story. I once met Louie Giglio, the influential author and leader at Passion City Church in Atlanta, and I asked him, "How did you get on stage? I want to be a speaker." Without hesitating he replied, "I stayed."

I looked at him quizzically.

He then turned to my wife and said, "Do you know who LeBron James is?"

She laughed and said, "Of course I know who LeBron James is."

"Look at LeBron's career. He could've played football as well as a lot of other sports, but he found his gift and fully committed to it. He stayed." When you and I stay, that is when we have a greater opportunity to reach what Louie calls "maximum capacity." Wouldn't you like to say that you reached maximum capacity on this planet?

We are so obsessed in this country with where we are going, with getting from Point A to Point B, but there's something profound about *staying* in God's embrace, leaning into our gifts, and constantly growing in self-awareness, to achieve the max capacity that God wants for us. You might not know how your life will unfold. You might not know where your transformation will take you. But I invite you to *stay* with Step 4 and spend time with it almost every day—to take a "searching and fearless moral inventory" with curiosity and compassion. This journey inward will be the fuel to your continual transformation. Congratulations on embarking on this very vital step.

Scan the QR code to watch a special message from Bart about Chapter Four.

CHAPTER 5

RADICALLY REAL

I hadn't talked to my mom in several weeks. I was embarrassed. I didn't want her to know I was in rehab. I didn't want her to know that her son "had a problem." My mom and I always talked about green grass and high tides. We didn't talk about Dad's alcoholism in my childhood, so why would we talk about mine? We both had a way of brushing difficult conversations under the rug. Discussing something like accountability or shortcomings would've involved acknowledging the unresolved, complicated things in life. Whenever I wrecked another car in high school, I remember Mom saying to me, "Don't tell your grandmother." Accountability was feared because of how messy it was.

I think one of the reasons my family avoided difficult conversations was a generational factor. People didn't always voice their grief back then. They just worked harder. Mom was discontent after my dad died but made up for it with hard work and positivity—not a bad response to life's challenges. When Dad was living, Mom got her pilot's license, something women did not do back then. She wanted to make sure she was comfortable flying a plane just in case something happened to Dad while they were in the air. When Dad passed away, she took over the dealership, probably the only woman in the country running a dealership at that time.

Mom and I had a good relationship—it got better in later years—but I certainly never told her about the ugliness of my lifestyle and the terrible decisions I was making. She had no idea I was living the way I was living. Instead I told her about how much money I was bringing in and all the vehicles we owned and the influential people we knew. I was just putting perfume on the pig, masking my deepest pain with success.

But in recovery, my values began to change. Two weeks into rehab—in the middle of going through classes and meetings—I went into the bathroom and noticed something in the pocket of my button-down shirt: a small bag of cocaine. Apparently I had forgotten to remove it from one of my work shirts when I packed my bag for rehab. Was it a subconscious slip? A safety net I wanted to give myself in case sobriety was too much to handle?

I removed the bag from my pocket. I held it in my hand, almost shaking, my compulsion raging. I thought about how good it would feel to do a line. I thought about how confident it would make me feel at a time when my confidence was shattered. I thought about the high that would momentarily rescue me from this low point in my life.

But then I thought about all I had been learning. I thought about my emotional connection to cocaine. I thought about the dead-end this drug had brought me to. I played out my compulsion and remembered how miserable I would feel inside if I caved to the pressure. I thought about my parents' work ethic, particularly Mom's, and how I would need to tap into that same drive and commitment if I was ever going to change and get sober.

I set the bag on the bathroom counter. I looked in the mirror—deep into the eyes of the man I had always been ashamed of, who had gravitated toward any sign of attention and affection since high school, who had always sought to become someone who he wasn't. I again admitted I was powerless, that I could be restored, and made a decision to turn my life over. Remember when my counselor Gus said I would never make it?

I went into a stall, flushed the bag of cocaine down the toilet, and remember saying out loud, "Take that, Gus."

At that moment, it was as if the Red Sea parted before my eyes. Just a couple weeks before I had lost my job when my boss caught me snorting cocaine in the bathroom. Now I was flushing it into the past. I had chosen the direction I was going to go. I had decided to choose freedom, to focus my energy on rescuing myself from this addiction I had been enslaved to. I had gotten real with myself and decided I was going to make decision after decision after decision to heal. I knew at that point there was no turning back. I had been around people who had relapsed, but now I had proven to myself that I could look my greatest temptation in the eye and walk away. It felt *good* to walk away, to choose something deeper beyond temporary pleasure. I didn't realize it at the time but what I was ultimately choosing was a deeper relationship with God each time I turned from my temptation. I was partnering with transformation. I was making a decision (there it is, Step 3 again) that there was more value in *keeping* the change rather than caving to my vice.

It may have been later that day or the next that I finally decided to give my mom a call. If I was going to get real with myself about the intensity of my addiction, then I also had to get real with the people in life I loved the most. I had to quit putting perfume on the pig and admit to others *exactly* where I had gone wrong. I knew that what I was about to tell her was the exact opposite of the success my family idolized. I was jobless, in a strained marriage that was hurtling toward divorce, and in recovery for both cocaine and alcohol. The son who she had lovingly raised was leading a life that was broken to the core.

I dialed her number. She picked up immediately, as she always did. As I shared with her the truth—the complicated mess I had made of my life—I think she was scared but also proud. It was as if I was I was paving a different way for our family—one that was marked by radical realness rather than masking our pain with success—while also trying to tap into the work ethic she had modeled for me her entire life.

Mom became my most supportive companion on the journey. Just as she never missed a swim meet of mine in high school, she wouldn't miss an AA birthday of mine until the age of ninety-seven when she stepped into heaven.

The fifth step of Celebrate Recovery reads, "We admitted to God, to ourselves, and to another human being the exact nature of our wrongs." It's one thing to do the fourth step—to take a fearless moral inventory of oneself—but this can begin and end with private introspection. If we don't get honest with others, our transformation can be devoid of accountability and community, which is *essential* to lifelong change.

That's why recovery meetings work. At a meeting, each person admits their addiction to all in attendance. Your social class doesn't matter. Your job or lack of one doesn't matter. The car you drove to the meeting or the home you'll return to after the meeting doesn't matter. Everyone's journey has brought them to this vulnerable place—this humble, broken state which makes authentic relationship possible. Addicts at a recovery meeting recognize they are on a level playing field, are united in their brokenness, and are accountable to one another through the power of vulnerability.

This is also why Christianity—*when* believers are actually honest and real with one another—can be so impactful. Christians are united not only in Christ's love for each individual person but also in their own brokenness or humanness. Everyone misses the mark and is in need of some type of change. The key is whether Christians dare (or anyone else for that matter) to be honest about the exact nature of our wrongs. Many people prefer instead to use religion as a self-righteous mask (remember the Johari Window?) instead of a direct route to being vulnerable. The great thing about a relationship with Jesus is that it's exactly that: it's a relationship with the King of the universe, and it's not about rituals or rules.

Pastor Craig Groeschel once said that a key to leadership is being relentlessly real instead of having to be right. In being authentically real, we open ourselves up to connect with others in our own vulnerability and transparency. But when we are so focused on being right, our egos construct walls that trap us in our own self-centered chamber and push others out. If what you believe in doesn't involve loving or serving others, your belief is far too shallow.

Vulnerability is key to honesty and integrity. Paul, who likely wrestled with his past sins of killing and persecuting Christians before his conversion on the road to Damascus, models vulnerability in Corinthians 12:9-10: "But he said to me, 'My grace is sufficient for you, for my power is made perfect in weakness.' Therefore I will boast all the more gladly about my weaknesses, so that Christ's power may rest on me. That is why, for Christ's sake, I delight in weaknesses, in insults, in hardships, in persecutions, in difficulties. For when I am weak, then he is strong."

Have you ever heard someone talk about "sin" and immediately check out of the conversation? In our culture, we're allergic to words like "sin." I know I was. As an unchurched person, a counselor referred to sin as simply missing the mark. When you see the word "sin," even though it isn't necessarily a word we like or use, it means we missed the mark; that we're not living up to our max capacity. This is also why Christianity can be so impactful.

Naming the exact nature of our wrongs—our *sin*—to both God and others is one of the most difficult of the 12 Steps. "Boasting in our weaknesses" goes directly against putting perfume on the pig (living in pride). Pride is all about boosting the ego and protecting the ego. Vulnerability is about nourishing the soul. When we dare to share our weaknesses mutually with someone else, each person is reminded that they aren't alone in their deepest struggles; that intimate connection is more important than masking our pain; and that we are accountable to one another as we change together.

I remember once telling my son about a fight my wife and I had and sharing with him the "exact nature of my wrongs," thinking that I was being honest and transparent. He stopped me in the middle of my word vomiting and said, "Dad, I don't need to know that. Talk to your sponsor about that." This is where integrity comes in. When I word vomited all over my son in the name of "honesty," I was actually just looking for someone to make me feel better about myself; someone to alleviate my guilt; someone to project everything upon so I could check "honesty" off my list and move on with my day. That's *not* honesty because there is something about this bizarre form of scapegoating that lacks integrity.

Vulnerability *isn't* about centering ourselves and talking about our weaknesses. As my son said, "Talk to your sponsor." It just means that we have a team around us who we can confide in about our hurts, habits, and hang-ups. Sometimes vulnerability might mean saying, "I'm sorry," or, "I was wrong," or, "I was short with you yesterday, and that's not okay."

We need to remember that "working the steps" isn't a formula we use just to help us feel better about ourselves. Authentically engaging the steps involves honest introspection. Had I taken a *fearless* moral inventory before projecting my junk upon my son, I would have uncovered that there was lingering guilt that I needed to process with his mom, not him. Fearlessness involves leaning into that darkness and exploring it. What was happening beneath the surface? What was I really craving? What would be the most healthy, holistic, and honest step forward?

Data dumping always creates a thunderstorm. The human condition is so weird, isn't it? Even something as transformative as the 12 Steps can become hijacked by ego. What do I mean? They can be used as a self-righteous mask. They can become watered down and turned into a surface-level mechanism for alleviating guilt rather than genuine, messy transformation. Even something like "authenticity" can be used to make money or craft a fake persona on social media that is the exact opposite of "real."

But when done right, Step 5 propels us forward further into our own healing. In rehab, they talk a lot about the three H's: *honesty*, *humility*, and *help*. I had no idea how to be honest until rehab. I was a car salesmen, refined in my ability to embellish. If I sold twenty cars one month, I'd tell Mom that I sold twenty-five. This is still something I battle. The other day I caught myself telling someone that I was in Hawaii with my kids for three weeks. No, I wasn't. I was there for ten days. But when we choose to be honest about our own life circumstances, we position ourselves to become radically real. We leave the myths we've been believing behind. We accept our lives as they are. This honesty and humility paves the path toward help. Without honesty and humility we can't get the help we need because our deepest needs remain buried beneath the surface. Honesty and humility position us to *name* the truth so that others can come alongside us and help us heal—and eventually we can help others heal. Accountability is where integrity flourishes.

Every evening I ask myself three questions and journal about them: *What did I do right? What did I learn? What must I change?* This exercise brings Step 4 and Step 5 together for me. The questions guide me inward to evaluate my life and then invite me to *name* what is happening beneath the surface. When taken seriously, this exercise cultivates the three H's within my heart: honesty, humility, and help.

Notice, too, how the questions begin by guiding us toward positivity and curiosity rather than judgment or self-condemnation. Depending on your personality, the 12 Steps or any method of self-development for that matter can sometimes open wounds that cause us to beat ourselves up. On a day that I'm being particularly hard on myself, I still can't move on to the second question until I'm honest with the first: *What did I do right today?* Maybe I messed up big time that day. Maybe I can't stop replaying my mistakes in my head. No matter, I'm not allowed to evaluate those mistakes until I first take time to praise myself for the things I did right. Just as good parents should affirm their children more than they criticize them, we should do the same thing with ourselves.

Studies show that our brains tend to cling to negativity or circumstances that lack resolve. When we ask ourselves what we did right, we are programming ourselves to look for the right, not the wrong. We are conditioning our minds. We are what we focus on. When we get negative, the truth is that we would never talk to someone else the way we talk to ourselves.

Only after the first question is honestly addressed can we move onto the second question: *What did I learn?* In this we might find ourselves reflecting on aspects of our day that did not go quite how we anticipated. But even these moments entail conscious reframing. The question is not, "Why am I a failure?" I choose to believe there is no such thing as failure if we are genuinely learning from it. In answering this question we are invited to be gentle with ourselves and reframe our mistakes as our greatest teachers. Tony Robbins says there is no such thing as failure; there is only results. When we ask this question, "What did I learn?" we can change the results. John Maxwell has a book called *Sometimes You Win, Sometimes You ~~Lose~~ Learn.* That sums it up, doesn't it? We might not always win, but if we ask ourselves a great question, that's how we take ownership of our path.

If we're not learning, we aren't changing. We can get a gauge on our level of integrity by the depth of our change, by the substance of our transformation. As a Christian, I believe that integrity begins by realizing how much God loves us, which inspires a love for God, ourselves, and others. So, if our answer to this question does not reflect this love for God, ourselves, and others, then the answer already lacks integrity. For example, if I embarrassed myself in a work meeting that morning and answer this question that night with, "I learned that I'm a stupid idiot and should keep my mouth shut," that answer lacks integrity because it doesn't cultivate love and compassion for myself. It doesn't reflect the way God sees me as a child who He loves. A better way to answer the question might be, "I learned that sometimes I don't listen as well as I should and am too quick to respond." If we're being hard on ourselves—beating ourselves to a pulp—then we're not honoring Christ in us. I see this all the time in the people who I sponsor. One time I asked a sponsee who just could not stop beating himself up, "If you think so low of yourself, then why would you listen to yourself in the first place?" Another thing Tony says is that the quality of our life is determined by the quality of our questions. That's why we *have* to reframe our questions.

The third question I ask at the end of the day is, *What must I change?* This can launch us into the next day with purpose and conviction. Whereas the first two questions are more reflective of Step 4 and Step 5—introspectively taking a moral inventory and naming what needs to be done—this question launches us back into the fundamental actions of the first three steps: *admitting, believing,* and *deciding.* We admit what it is we want to change; we believe in a power greater than ourselves that can help us change; and we make a decision in answering this question *to* change. There's no point even trying to answer this question if we aren't stirred to change. The question does not say, *What do I **want** to change?* It says, *What **must** I change?* Wanting is not enough for authentic transformation. Tony says, "If you must, you will. If you can't, you must." Sick of Tony yet?

We have to *need* to change. That's how strong our conviction has to be. If we can cultivate a hunger for change with the intensity of an addict's desire to stay sober, we will find ourselves constantly evolving. You don't have to be an addict to cultivate the hunger, but we MUST cultivate the hunger, whether an addict or not. We have to *trust* that the help is out there for us to change if we open ourselves up and become radically real. As speaker Les Brown says, for us to have success in any area of our life, "You've gotta be hungry!"

In our introspection, these questions take us beyond the black-and-white labels of a "good day" or "bad day;" of "winning or "losing;" of "success" or "failure." They invite us to get serious about what it is we would like to change and truly consider what it will take to do it. We need to remember that there's something so human about mistakes, regret, and failure. As a Christian, I believe there's only one person to walk this planet without making a mistake: Jesus. If you meet someone who acts like they never make mistakes, you can almost bet that they aren't transforming. Our mistakes signal to us what needs to change, but we must become vulnerable about them.

Honesty. Humility. Help.

There is victory in voicing what is beneath the surface. As we become vulnerable enough to get help, we take control of our lives, no longer directed by things we've yet to acknowledge. As Carl Jung once wrote, "Until you make the unconscious conscious, it will direct your life and you will call it fate."

Scan the QR code to watch a special message from Bart about Chapter Five.

CHAPTER 6

RUM-LAYERED SOUP

T wo weeks after the cocaine-in-the-bathroom incident, I graduated from the recovery center. My family decided to celebrate
at a high-end restaurant in Monterey, California, called the Sardine
Factory, a famous spot with eclectic decor and wonderful food. We
were guided to our seat, and I ordered a bowl of lobster bisque. One
spoonful was all it took. I spit it out all over the table, probably embarrassing my family as well as everyone in the restaurant.

I tasted rum on the top of the soup.

In my time in the recovery program, they hammer home that there
is no such thing as easing back into drinking or using or whatever it
was that brought you to recovery. For alcoholics there's no such thing
as drinking in moderation. The addict has to establish a firm boundary
that entails no compromises. They have to have the humility to know
that one sip, one thought, or even a half ounce of rum in lobster bisque
can set them off.

Spitting out my soup was my line in the sand. I went through the
house and found all the bags of cocaine I had hid—beneath sofa cush-
ions, buried in closet corners, stuffed in shirt pockets. I also collected
every bottle of alcohol from the kitchen and garage. I flushed each bag
of cocaine down the toilet. I poured every bottle of alcohol down the
drain. Though I could have just thrown it all away, there was something
symbolic about pouring each bottle and flushing each bag. The steady
glug-glug-glug of each bottle being poured. The dispersing of the powder.

63

All that money I had spent. All the wild nights those bottles and bags could fuel. Every emotional attachment I had to both substances. Not even one sip was worth risking the downward spiral that would follow.

Tony Robbins says that if you have enough pain, you'll change. If you put your finger on a hot stove, you'll pull it off as quickly as possible. Addicts have to know that there is *nothing* worth compromising because the potential pain is so unbearable. We already know the stove is scorching hot, so why even put our finger close to it?

I still had a lot to learn about both myself and God, but all I knew at that point in my journey was that I *hated* my past life and was determined to never go back there again. I'd have to learn to sell cars and manage people sober, which, sad to say, was foreign to me. I'd have to fill my evenings with something other than partying. I'd have to put boundaries up in previous relationships. No more hanging out with my buddy who smoked crack. No more going to the bar with co-workers after work. No more putting myself in social situations where I'd be tempted to slip back into my old ways.

To help with this radical transition, I followed the advice from rehab and went to ninety recovery meetings in ninety days. That philosophy in recovery is known as "one day at a time." The only reason I got to the place I am now is because I took it one day at a time. As the saying goes, "Yesterday is history, tomorrow is a mystery, today is a gift. That's why they call it the present." The meetings helped me learn to focus on *today*.

Those meetings especially helped reinforce Step 5 (hopefully you are beginning to see by now how the steps begin to run into one another or unfold simultaneously). The meetings were reminders that I was not alone in my addiction, though many days felt isolating. If they could do it, then I could too. When you start to believe the lie that you're a lone ranger on this journey, that's usually where the darkness starts to creep in. Gathering among others who were seeking victory over their addiction reminded me of the community I both needed and craved.

One of the most amazing things about this new life I had chosen was the realization that my time, energy, and resources could be harnessed toward more meaningful things. When you're in the thick of your addiction, you don't realize just how much you're giving to fuel it. The time I spent each day partying and drinking. The ridiculous amounts of money I was spending on cocaine and alcohol. The physical depleted-ness, hangover headaches, and all I had to do to get back to a state of normalcy.

Going *all-in* on fighting unhealthy patterns makes space for new, healthy, more meaningful habits to emerge.

I had a marriage that was probably beyond repair but needed healing. A year before sobriety, our daughter was born. One year later, we had a son. Five years later, we would have twin boys. Through all of that, I still had a lot of maturing to do when it came to being a husband, but I discovered that I *loved* being a present father. Now that I wasn't partying and drinking I learned that I *could* be someone whom my dad was not. Though my dad wasn't very engaged, I could be massively engaged. I could be present. I even found out that I actually liked selling cars and managing people sober. I felt more stable, more authentic, more dependable. I started to like myself a little bit. I had begun the journey of learning to love myself.

Accepting my disease and operating within certain parameters each day allowed the most meaningful things in my life to expand. No, sobriety was not a quick fix. All was not healed internally for me. In fact, within my new lifestyle boundaries, unresolved tensions within myself rose to the surface. But rather than masking them with a hurt, habit, or hangup, I was finally equipped to *deal* with them. Acceptance led to discipline, and discipline was leading to transformation—the old to the new.

The sixth step of Celebrate Recovery reads, "We were entirely ready to have God remove all these defects of character." *Entirely ready* is the key phrase in Step 6. Our readiness is what positions us for the journey and it's something we must return to again and again. Perhaps you've heard an alcoholic correct anyone who labels them as "someone who used to be an alcoholic." Addicts know that there is no "used to be." The second we think it is behind us is the second we let down our guard. In spiritual language, the second we become content or lukewarm is the second we give the devil a foothold. Our past addiction, suddenly, becomes one of our greatest gifts. It keeps us humble. It keeps us open to be shaped and molded. The Steps continually welcome us back to the journey of transformation.

But we have to truly *accept* that our past lifestyle offers no value anymore. Our discipline reflects the depth of our acceptance and readiness. Going *all-in* on ridding ourselves of our unhealthy patterns as they pertain to our addictions or attachments is how we show God that we are ready to partner with Him on the journey of transformation. This sanctification process is how God makes us into the person and servant leader we were designed to be. We are all "in process" of becoming new creations. As Paul wrote in 2 Corinthians 5:17, "Therefore, if anyone is in Christ, the new creation has come: The old has gone, the new is here!" I had to die to my old behavior.

The New Testament talks a lot about the notion of being "born again"—the idea that if we put to death our unhealthy patterns, that if we have "crucified the flesh with its passions and desires" (Galatians 5:24), then we are born anew in Christ. What does this mean? As someone is dunked in the water, it's symbolism for the old self being buried and the new self being born. As Romans 6:4 says, "We were therefore buried with him through baptism into death in order that, just as Christ was raised from the dead through the glory of the Father, we too may live a new life." Recovery echoed the symbolism of baptism. New thinking. New habits. Thus, new behaviors and results.

Choosing to make difficult decisions—to "leave it behind"—will most likely feel like a little death. It will feel like you are being emptied. It might feel deeply uncomfortable, like you are cutting off your life-source. In a way, you are. You're going through a divorce—experiencing an intense split from your own unhealthy patterns; patterns that you think you need to survive. The more you accept your condition, the more you'll put to death passions and desires that are related to the addiction or attachment. It might feel scary. It might feel lonely. There might be dark days in the tomb, but trust and believe that on the other side is resurrection. A new life.

Like religion, the Steps, too, can sometimes become ultra-performance focused. As I've mentioned a couple times now, they can become the mechanism through which we beat ourselves up for our lacking performance—for every little way in which we are failing in life. Hopefully by now you can sense the importance of having a safety net on this journey when you slip and fall: abiding in God's grace and returning to self-compassion. Before we adopt a readiness for change and acceptance of what needs to change, we first must be ready to be accepted. If our self-esteem is low, we'll keep spiraling because we'll think we don't deserve the benefits of a new life.

As I've talked about before, that's why it's important to have a sponsor or life coach. I talked to my sponsor every day during my first couple years of sobriety. He wouldn't judge me but would hold me accountable to my behavior. He was what I needed at the time. I've sought out other sponsors who would be tougher on me. I've found that I've always needed a kick in the butt. Wayne Dyer says that "when the student is ready, the teacher will appear." One thing I've learned as a coach, church counselor, and mental health coach is that people really do want to change. The question is: Will they do what it takes to change?

There's a saying in AA that progress is what we should focus on, not perfection. Yes, performance *is* important and is something that should be stressed in Step 6. We're reminded in James 2:14 that faith without works is dead. But if you're having a hard time accepting yourself or don't feel like your life has forward motion, simply do what Jesus teaches in the book of Matthew: *pick up your mat and walk.* What that means for you and me is that we need to do the work and do it to the best of our ability, but this is not about being perfect. It's about moving our feet and doing what we need to do to be freed from our past behaviors. Love yourself in that journey of progress and know that only one person who ever walked this planet was perfect. That's what acceptance is all about — it's about loving yourself.

There's a quote from the *Big Book of Alcoholics Anonymous* that I love. It's long but worth meditating upon: "Acceptance is the answer to all my problems today. When I am disturbed, it is because I find some person, place, thing or situation—some fact of my life—unacceptable to me, and I can find no serenity until I accept that person, place, thing or situation as being exactly the way it is supposed to be at this moment. Nothing, absolutely nothing, happens in God's world by mistake. Until I could accept my alcoholism, I could not stay sober; unless I accept life completely on life's terms, I cannot be happy. I need to concentrate not so much on what needs to be changed in the world as on what needs to be changed in me and my attitudes."

Our works, our deeds, the steps forward we take in moving away from our past behaviors reflect how ready we are to change and our acceptance of what we need to change. Again, if we're struggling to change, then maybe we don't hate our sin enough. Sin, as a reminder, is simply missing the mark. Maybe we are using grace as a crutch instead of an animating force for authentic change.

What is grace? It's another one of those words we hear in the church, but what does it mean for you and me? Grace is receiving what we don't deserve. God has given us wonderful gifts that we don't deserve, but they were still given. That's grace. God says that he loves us no matter what. Moved by this love and grace we have freely received, we naturally want to change our thinking and do good works. God has given each of us new opportunities even when we didn't deserve them.

Believer or not, each of us is invited into this new life on the other side of our addictions and attachments. But we have to see the rich value in this new life—the freedom new habits would provide, the peace we would experience, and the capacity we have to love when our hurts, habits, and hangups aren't sucking our energy like a leach. If we can't sense that, if we can't *taste* that, we might not be entirely ready to let God remove our defects of character.

But if you've made it this far in the book, I would bet that you're ready. That you're aware of your character defects. That you've accepted who you are and *whose* you are despite these embarrassing failures: someone who is loved, chosen, and ready for a new life. And that you're now *ready* to shift, to change, to establish boundaries, to cut out unhealthy relationships, to create new accountability partners, to confide in your sponsor, to create new habits, and ultimately taste the peace that expands the more freedom we experience from our addictions. Peace is found by not being tormented by our addictions.

I once sponsored a man who spent most of our sessions complaining about how his life had gone wrong. His children hated him. He couldn't hold a steady job. He had all kinds of physical issues related to his addiction, including early signs of emphysema from smoking two packs of cigarettes a day. He told me he was yet to stay sober from alcohol for more than three months despite the fact he had been going to meetings for twenty years. One of the things he refused to do, I noticed, was throw away the bottles of alcohol he kept in his apartment. I could tell that part of him wanted to get sober, hence his several two-month-long streaks of sobriety, but the other part of him hated himself so much he believed he deserved to live a miserable life, one of the reasons why he kept alcohol in his home. He was caught in a negative feedback loop that went on and on and on, predictably playing itself out every few months. My heart ached seeing someone who had such a low self-esteem. I had been there myself and honestly still go back there sometimes, haunted by my past behaviors. I could tell my friend was stuck and would remain stuck until he changed his response to the events of his life. Frankly, there wasn't much I could do as his sponsor until he worked these first six steps (starting with Step 1!) and was *entirely ready* to change.

This might be an extreme example, but this is all of us to some degree, isn't it? Most of us fear, on some level, what is on the other side of change. Most of us fear what life will be like if we make a clean break with our addictions or attachments. Many of us are so discouraged by how our lives have unfolded that we've lost our desire *to* change. But don't let anyone ever tell you that it's too late to change. Until I'm no longer breathing, I plan on changing, transforming, growing. If God can make someone like Abraham, in his old age, the father of all nations, then God is not done with you. Here I am, when some people retire, feeling like my life and career is starting over. Writing this book. Growing as a public speaker. Beginning again.

In Jack Canfield's popular book *The Success Principles,* he teaches about a very valuable formula that can help us to evaluate our decision-making and position us to be *entirely ready* to change: E+R=O.

*Event + **Response** = **Outcome***

Canfield frames this formula as something that can put us in control of our destiny, ushering us to take *full* responsibility of our lives. The basic idea, he says, is that every outcome, whether it be success or failure, is a result of how we respond to an event. Think about it. There is only one thing we *can* control, and that is our *response* to life's events. Therefore, changing our futures requires changing our responses. But most people, Canfield says, blame the *event* (in other words, they play the victim and say "why me?" instead of "what is my role in this?") when they're disappointed with an outcome and bypass evaluating how they responded to the event.

Think about it. You're driving down the road, and you get cut off. You can get dramatic and chase them down and run them off the road.

The outcome, of course, is that you go to jail. Or you can just focus on your breathing and turn your music up and go on with your day.

So, how do we change our responses? How do we break the cycle when our lives have become Groundhog's Day? A good starting point would be evaluating our own self-image. One of my favorite quotes of all-time is from Maxwell Maltz's *Psycho-Cybernetics,* "You can never outperform your own self-image." Let's pause and really let those words resonate.

> *You can never outperform*
> *your own self image.*

Our responses to events are directly related to how we view ourselves, which affects the outcomes. Another friend of mine, Dr. Harold Bafitis, once said something similar regarding plastic surgery—that when you change a person on the outside, it affects how they might see themselves on the inside, impacting how they interact with their world. On the other hand, he found that some people kept repeatedly coming in for plastic surgery because the way they viewed themselves on the inside never changed. Their insecurities always called the shots, and they obsessed over their outside image. The class I teach on Self Image Mastery is an opportunity to really look at oneself through the course of an in-depth, six-month program.

We are not born with ideas or insecurities. Our ideas and insecurities come from our experiences in life and our perception of those experiences. These ideas and insecurities deserve careful evaluation because they inevitably affect our own self-image, which impacts our responses to events. My whole mission in life is giving other people hope. In other words, Helping Other People Expand. When we dare to see our inherent potential longing to burst forth from our hearts and minds to positively impact the world, we'll find ourselves not only ready but *eager* to deal with our character defects.

I want to conclude this chapter with a quote from the aforementioned book, *The Greatest Salesman in the World* by Og Mandino. The fourth of the ten scrolls is one of my favorites. It says that you are "nature's greatest miracle." I invite you to take these words to heart: "I am not on this earth by chance. I am here for a purpose and that purpose is to grow into a mountain, not to shrink to a grain of sand.

Henceforth I will apply all my efforts to become the highest mountain of all and I will strain my potential until it cries for mercy...I am nature's greatest miracle."

Scan the QR code to watch a special message from Bart about Chapter Six.

CHAPTER 7
ANCHORED AND OPEN

There are many alcoholics who get sober and then think their problems are in the rearview mirror. Wait a minute. There are many *humans* who get to the other side of something difficult and think their problems are in the rearview mirror. Again, please don't think this book is *just* for alcoholics or addicts. For the nineteenth time, I'm reminding you.

Anyway, on one level, it's kind of true: most people who struggle with addiction never gain the courage to go to recovery and get sober. Sobriety and self-healing *are* a big deal and *should* be celebrated. It's a heroic, daring act that leads to the greatest feeling of victory one can experience in this lifetime. My sobriety was a breakthrough in my own development. We are all in the process of healing, no matter our hurts, habits, or hangups.

Chad Moore, the lead pastor at Sun Valley Church, has installed Celebrate Recovery at many of their church campuses. Why? After experiencing a betrayal that turned his life upside down, he turned to CR even though he wasn't an addict. He says that CR is for everybody and those who don't think it's for them are in denial.

What you begin to see in CR is that your addictions, hurts, habits, and hangups are often symptoms for a deeper problem. Many addicts realize even in their sobriety that their addictive tendencies come out in other ways. Or, having begun their journey of self-awareness, now equipped with the steps for change, their eyes are opened to other toxic patterns they need to confront. I wish I could tell you that my life was rosy after I got sober. I wish I could tell you that everything clicked into place. But it didn't. For most people, it doesn't. The truth is that nearly two straight decades of partying and narcissistic behaviors will leave your maturity severely stunted. What they say with alcoholics is that if you started drinking at thirteen and stopped at forty, you're still thirteen years old—you're emotionally stunted.

I had a lot to learn. By now I hope you realized that having a lot to learn simply means that there are many more victories to be won.

Picture driving through the mountains on a long road trip and encountering a tunnel blocked from a rockslide. Drugs and alcohol were like a road block on my journey. Just because I "worked hard" to clear the tunnel didn't mean I had arrived at my destination. In fact, I had a long ways to go. After twenty years of going nowhere, my journey was beginning again. I was realizing the deeper effects of my own "stinking thinking."

In my first decade of sobriety, my life and capacity to love undoubtedly expanded in my freedom from drugs and alcohol, those symptoms of my own self-sabotaging. There's no denying that. I became a better father, friend, and leader. As my daughter, son, and twin boys began going to school and playing sports, I never missed a school function or sporting event. Sobriety, without a doubt, positioned me to be more present. In this sense, victory over alcohol and drugs led me to the greatest gift I could ever give.

But I'll be honest with you: my addiction to attention and affection remained. I remained relationally (and romantically) stunted. I had a long ways to go on *that* journey. I made *better* decisions without being under the influence of drugs and alcohol, but chasing the next pleasure remained my *modus operandi*. I did not stop flirting. I snuck around in the shadows. I had a warped sense of attention and affection.

Did I feel guilty? Absolutely, and my self-esteem was in the tank. But my faith was shallow. I had strict morals with drugs and alcohol, but for some reason those ethics were yet to expand into other areas of my life. I guess you could say that I made the mistake that a lot of addicts make. My confidence (and even pride, perhaps) in my sobriety made me falsely think that the war was won when in fact drugs and alcohol was just a battle. I had cleared the tunnel from the rockslide yet I still proverbially sat still in my car going nowhere, or perhaps moved up the road very slowly. I had a clear road ahead of me but struggled to engage transformation fully.

One Sunday morning, I drove past a church in Santa Cruz, CA and saw several Mercedes Benz in the parking lot. My interest was piqued. Leave it to me to get curious about church because of the cars I saw in the lot. Maybe church was what my life was missing. Maybe *faith* was what my life was missing. The Adrian Center had led me to the doorstep of prayer and, in a sense, depending on God—my "Source"—for my sobriety, but I was far from a committed Christian. In fact, I'm not sure if I knew what a Christian was. I was curious about who God was and getting to know him, but I wasn't sure what that meant. What I *did* know is that chasing attention and affection left me feeling empty and angry.

I'll always remember walking into that church in Santa Cruz and feeling like I was home. I quickly realized it had nothing to do with the cars in the parking lot! They were just there to get my attention. I loved that there were no thees and thous being shouted from the pulpit. People were relatable, dressed in jeans and t-shirts, with seemingly nothing to prove or hide. The worship band played rock and roll, their music pulsing with energy, a true celebration of God's love and grace. The congregation seemed to realize that being there was more about the heart's experience, not the ego's experience of appearing self-righteous or "having it all together" (the vibe I sometimes got from church goers). The pastor, Chip Ingram, was an incredible communicator who was convicting but not preachy.

I began attending church every week. What I've learned is that God loves us so much that He will even use our egos or sin to lead us to Him; to love; to peace; to freedom. I began reading Scripture every day. I got involved in Celebrate Recovery. God helped me to press my foot down on the pedal and engage transformation. The introspection that began at the Adrian Center years before was taken to an even deeper level. I began to feel conviction to live a more pure life, a more grounded life. God exposed every defect of my character (ouch), just as the Adrian Center had exposed my addiction. I was again being invited into transformation and began traveling down the road toward victory.

❖❖❖

The seventh step of Celebrate Recovery says that "We humbly asked

God to remove all our shortcomings." What's a shortcoming? It's those things that are stopping you from becoming your best self. The key word here is *all* and indicates a turning point in the steps. Whereas the first six steps were focused on the pain as it relates to our addiction, now we are humbly asking God to remove *all* our shortcomings. We are invited to take the tools we learned in recovery—the wisdom we gained in experiencing freedom—and use those tools to continue our journey of self-awareness and transformation…in *every* area of our lives. "Sick and tired of being sick and tired," the Seventh Step invites us into a lifelong journey of change that continually expands. As the Big Book says, if you don't gain humility then you will be humiliated. Developing our spiritual selves—our inner lives—is directly related to a person's capacity for humility. When I learned that, my life started to change dramatically.

Faith, at its best, is fuel as we press down on the pedal and continue our journey of becoming who and whose we were made to be. As I started attending church regularly, I quickly realized that the conviction I felt about alcohol and drugs began to extend into other areas of my life. Sexual integrity. Controlling my anger. Leading with selfless service. Treating others as I would like to be treated. Of course, this transformation didn't happen immediately. Transformation can take decades, especially when there are established negative habits from your "zombie days." Those are hard to purge.

Along with the Third Step prayer, I began to get on my knees every morning and pray the Seventh Step prayer. It goes like this, "My Creator, I am now *willing* that you should have all of me, good and bad. I pray that you now remove from me every single defect of character which stands in the way of my usefulness to you and my fellows. Grant me strength, as I go out from here, to do your bidding. Amen." *Willing* is the key word there. We can't be willing without being anchored in humility. We can't be willing if we aren't open to change. Our defects block our usefulness. The more we allow God to remove these defects, the more effective we will be in our purpose. The more we partner with God in this process of inner transformation, through discipline and obedience, the more healthy and whole we will feel. Why? Because we are leaning more into the Holy Spirit work within us—our true self in Christ. Again, hopefully you're seeing how this doesn't just have to do with "addicts" but anyone who wants to live a life of significance. Some of you reading this are "normal" people, yet you're reading this and probably thinking, "I need to work these steps too."

In Step 3 we adopt a humble posture as we ask for help, but in Step 7 this humble posture becomes an animating force in our lives. I was once on a hockey trip with my kids. I was talking to another parent about sobriety and told her that every day I get on my knees and pray those two prayers from Step 3 and Step 7. A little confused, she asked me, "Why do you have to get on your knees?"

"Because for me, I have to *physically* demonstrate that I am giving my heart to God," I explained.

Opening ourselves up to sobriety and a way of life divorced from our addiction sets a new trajectory for us: for humility—asking for help, the definition of prayer—to establish positive, more healthy habits and patterns. This begins with bowing down to God and giving him our hearts every day as we desire to be more effective. Or, if the "God" word still rubs you the wrong way, then desiring to be a more purposeful human being. Simply put, as we allow Step 3 to expand into other avenues of our life, we arrive at Step 7.

Remove *all* our shortcomings? That can sound intimidating, can't it? How in the world can we expect ourselves to model perfect integrity? The truth is: we can't. But God can. We will never be perfect. We will always have baggage. We will always make mistakes. That is, again, where we need grace and love. That's who God is. Spiritual growth can slow if it's anchored in performance. We exhaust ourselves. We burn out. The truth is that we're not what we do; we're who God says that we are. As we humbly submit to God and ask him to remove every defect of character, as we expand our healthy habits, we must also try to see ourselves how God sees us: as loved, as whole, as full, as one of a kind, as designed for a purpose. Our new habits must be constructed upon the foundation of love and grace. If our identity is centered in our performance, not love and grace, then we'll have an identity crisis or risk spiraling into self-defeat every time we make a mistake. Being anchored in Christ is to say that we are anchored in love. As the Golden Rule says, "Love one another as you love yourselves." Well, as Storybrand founder Donald Miller once wrote, the Golden Rule assumes that you love and respect yourself. If you don't love yourself, how are you going to love others? Yes, there is always room to form new habits. But there is also always room for our God's loving view of us to transform our hearts one day at a time. The Twelve Steps move us to strengthen our discipline and obedience but to also anchor ourselves more and make us more like Him every day.

In Jesus's famous Parable of the Prodigal Son (Luke 15:11-32), we read about a rebellious son who essentially betrays his father by asking for his inheritance at a young age and leaving home. He squanders it on pleasure, or, one might say, on a warped sense of attention and affection—on addiction. The lost son eventually comes to his senses. He has his "Adrian Center" moment. He swallows his pride. He adopts a posture of humility for perhaps the first time. He returns home. As he approaches his father's house, we are told that his father sees the lost son on the path. The father *runs* toward the lost son and *embraces* him. His father has no pride. He has not been keeping score. He is happy to have his son home. In fact, it's his father's unconditional love and acceptance for the lost son, we can assume, that leads to the son's future obedience. When grace is *truly* received, we *act* upon that consuming love. That's what true love does: it leads to *deeper* commitment, and, in that commitment, love expands in even more mysterious, fulfilling ways.

I don't feel like someone can write the previous sentence without true transparency. My first marriage lasted twenty years but I was not exactly the consummate husband. We raised a beautiful family together—the best decision of my life—but our husband-and-wife relationship dissolved in my relentless chase for attention and affection. I didn't like myself or love myself, which made it difficult to be a reliable husband.

As I continued going to CR and learning about my hurts, habits, and hangups, I told myself that I wouldn't let myself get into a relationship until I was no longer bringing all my baggage from the past into the day-to-day ebbs and flows of a relationship. Of course, we all have baggage. I just didn't want a significant other to have to deal with carrying it every day. As I experienced more and more freedom, I met Mary.

I was hesitant to get into another relationship—especially a *Christian* relationship—because Christians can sometimes judge others for their pasts. But not my wife, Mary. We had a powerful love story that has not been without normal struggles. But we know how to get through them. We keep venturing deeper and deeper into commitment. I cannot speak for her, but for me, I have seen love expand the more I commit to what we have promised to one another. Even when I don't feel like it. Even when I'm frustrated. Even when our relationship is tumultuous. Even when I judge *myself* for my past. I am committed to our relationship. I keep anchoring myself in her love, even when I do not feel worthy to receive it. As I write this, we're on our seventh year of marriage. Between the two of us, we have ten kids and eleven grandkids.

We were recently asked by our church to teach a marriage class. At first I was overwhelmed with a sense of imposter syndrome. Who was *I* to teach a marriage class? But then I remembered about my step-father telling me about a successful company in Chicago that only hired executives who had lost a business in the past. Why? Because those executives knew what *not* to do; and knowing what not to do would help them know what to do moving forward. I thought about the time I fell asleep at the wheel in 2016 and ran into a pole (not drug or alcohol related, just sleep deprivation) and broke my foot. Doctors told me that when my foot healed it would be even stronger than before. On the first day of the marriage class I told them, "I'm in front of you not because I've been married fifty years. I've only been married seven years, and I know what not to do." And then I guided the class through the twelve steps in a marriage context…how I had to *admit* to the ways that I wasn't being a good spouse…how I had to *believe* that healing in this area was possible…how I had to *make a decision* to surrender this issue to God…how I had to *make a searching and fearless* inventory of my myself…how I had to *admit* the exact nature of my wrongs…how I had to be *entirely ready* to have God remove every defect of character… how I had to humbly *ask* God to remove all my shortcomings…etc.

Are you beginning to see how the twelve steps can be applied to transformation in any avenue of your life? Are you beginning to see how the twelve steps can cultivate commitment to the process? It's in this scope of commitment that we ask God to remove all our defects of character in every area of our lives. Because we are already consumed with God's love, we know it is safe to trust our darkness with Him and ask Him to invade it with light. We can, like the Prodigal Son, venture down the dusty road and let the Father's embrace alleviate us from our shame. We can commit our lives to this love that consumes and transforms us. We can let love remove *all* defects of character.

❖❖❖

This seventh step of Alcoholics Anonymous could not apply more to leadership.

We humbly ask God to remove all our shortcomings.

True leadership is humbly confronting one shortcoming after another. We must constantly ask: *Where are we being invited to grow? What is my role in this?* Leadership, after all, is a never-ending journey of growth. We never arrive. We keep learning. In being humble before both God and those who we are leading, we embrace curiosity and open our hearts and minds to feedback—the very avenue of our growth. In making a difficult decision, we know that we are going to have to make another difficult decision. This is what leadership is all about. This brings us back to the DISC assessment and the Johari Window. As we do the inner work to narrow our blindspots (which can only come through becoming more aware of our blindspots) and remove our facade (which can only come through honestly evaluating the masks we wear), we make room for our potential to expand. As we slowly confront the defects in our character and instill habits that speak to our blindspots, we lean more into our leadership potential. We also model curiosity and humility for those who we are leading.

The seventh step hinges upon continual openness to growth. Our openness is our anchor. It strengthens our confidence because we know we are growing; that we are on the right trajectory in life. We know that we do not have to have it all figured out; that it is not all up to us; that leadership will entail plenty of mistakes. We are on a journey. As John Maxwell says, "Growth is not an event." Growth is something that must be done consistently if you want to be a good leader, if you want to reach your max capacity as a human being; as a partner, as a friend, as a parent.

This is all a lot of work, but the reward on the other side is *amazing*. Growth is never-ending because of maintenance and constantly working on ourselves, but that means there are so many victories to be won. I went to a lot of counseling, for example. All the stuff I'm writing now came from counseling. When I was willing to talk about my hurts, habits, and hangups, their grip on me was loosened. When we're all willing to talk to others about our weaknesses, it loosens the grip our insecurities have on us. That's why I kept going to meetings even after I was so-called "sober."

Even now, after freedom from all this, I go to counseling. I have a coach. My coach focuses not on yesterday but today and tomorrow. A great counselor or coach asks awesome questions and listens. As I've heard it said, a man or woman convinced against their will is of the same opinion still. In other words, if you and I don't own the change, we won't change. It's one thing to know something or believe something; it's another thing to do it. Counseling and coaching help provide clarity in who we are and what our obstacles are. In 2013, I learned how to be a coach myself and enjoy coming alongside people as they navigate their hurts, habits, and hangups today.

Maxwell's Fifth Invaluable Law of Growth says that, "Motivation gets you going—discipline keeps you growing." Contentment is the enemy of growth. In the years that followed my graduation from the Adrian Center, I became comfortable in my sobriety. Yes, I attended meetings. Yes, I strengthened my boundaries with my addictive behaviors. Yes, all of this was a major feat. But freedom from hurts, habits, and hangups is not the end; it is the beginning of a growth journey that should unfold the rest of our lives. We must become "growth conscious"—aware of the different areas in our lives where we need to cultivate motivation and new areas where we need discipline.

What is an area in your life where you have a struggle but you've decided to not do anything about it? Maybe something that is simply too painful to deal with? Perhaps something you think that you cannot change? Or an unhealthy pattern in your life you've been doing for a long time and it's just who you are? Yes, personality has a lot to do with how you navigate your journey of transformation. But concluding "I'm just a passionate person" after yelling at an employee, or "I'm just introverted" whenever you make an employee feel guilty for bothering you, or "I'm just a perfectionist" after micromanaging an employee—these are all mere excuses that justify complacency. Excuses block our growth. They are also denial, and, once again, Denial is not a river in Egypt.

When it came to chasing attention and affection outside of marriage, I often justified my actions because of the festering issues in my previous relationship. I made excuses. I just "needed attention" or was just "getting even" or was just "doing the same thing others were doing." But justifications are often a sure sign that we have lost our way. No leader, no matter their personality, has room for excuses. As a leader, at home or in the workplace, it goes back to taking responsibility and being massively aware of our behavior.

Gaining awareness for our personalities and tendencies is a natural next step for cultivating humility. What are the things within myself that I don't understand? How can I gain an understanding for them that will help to serve people better? For example, according to the DISC, when I'm stressed, the D aspect of my personality—this desire to dominate and control—goes up. Frightened that, deep down, I feel so out of control, I construct a mask that makes people think I'm more in control than I actually am. This is why humility is fundamental to Step 7. If I think I don't have anything in my life that needs to change, that's a sign that I'm not being humble. I'm sure most people have had the experience of dating someone or working for someone who was never wrong and, thus, never apologized. This is usually because they are afraid of change; afraid to acknowledge that they have some inner work to do. In their minds, it's easier to just live in denial of the call to change or to blame others.

From what I've seen in coaching, low self-esteem also plays a factor. According to pastor Levi Lusko, we all have low self-esteem; we just show it differently than others.

When I was teaching a class based on Maxwell's twenty-one irrefutable laws of leadership, there was a question asking leaders to rank themselves on different virtues like humility. One guy laughed and said, "Can I rank myself a ten in humility?" If we have to say, we're humble, we're probably not. Get the point?

Step 7, to me, sits at the junction of all the other steps. It's fitting that it comes right in the middle of 12 Steps. It's almost as if the first six lead to Step 7 and the next six are built upon Step 7. Humility is core to working through each step, again and again, and keeping the change.

Scan the QR code to watch a special message from Bart about Chapter Seven.

CHAPTER 8
FLYING STAPLERS

John Maxwell writes that there are five levels of leadership: Position (Level 1), Permission (Level 2), Production (Level 3), People Development (Level 4), and Pinnacle (Level 5). Positional leadership, the lowest level, is when "leaders" rely on their position—their title—to often fear people into following. This might be the most common level of leadership, unfortunately. I'm sure you've seen someone climb the ranks and falsely think it's their "status" that gives them credibility to lead. This couldn't be further from the truth. A leader's connection with *people* and their ability to cultivate those people's gifts is what gives someone credibility to lead. The second level is relational leadership—a good step in the right direction—and is when people give someone *permission* to lead them because they trust the leader. The transition from Level 1 to Level 2 will be a big focus this chapter, as we move toward accountability and our connectedness to one another. Connection is what every other level of leadership is built upon. To be a coach is to help people with their hurts, habits, and hangups. That's what coaching is, and this is the missing link in today's culture that lacks good leadership. People aren't leaving companies. They're leaving people. It's not about the Xs and Os, it's about the Joanies and Joes. To give you a concept of what relational is, think about the customer service at Chik Fil A. I'm sure you've been to other fast food joints that you can tell are purely transactional.

When I was in the throes of my addiction, as well as the sober decade that followed before I found my faith, I would say that I was a Level 1 leader. I thought that my title is what gave me credibility to lead. It's embarrassing to say this, but I had very little interest in connecting with *people*, in truly investing in *relationships*; that is, unless there was an ulterior motive, say, landing a sale or chasing affection in some way. I usually liked the people I worked with, but my chief goal was always to sell product. Success was my idol. If someone wasn't hitting their benchmarks, then I lost respect for them. Work, to me, was all about the bottom line and increasing my personal wealth. Maybe one day I would get to the place where I could drive a Benz to church!

During those years there was always underlying anger that I would carry into the workplace, into my leadership position. In the first decade it was my use of drugs and alcohol that made me a deeply unhappy person. In the next it was my lack of integrity that always got me down, even though I didn't know what integrity looked like (that's where faith entered the picture). In either decade, I knew deep down that the way I was living didn't lead to peace. My continued chase for attention and affection was futile. Empty. Never enough to satisfy. I think this deep discontent usually came out in anger, as is the case for many men. As I've heard it said, anger is only a mask for sadness. My "Baby Bart" fits of rage usually unfolded in the workplace and at home.

One day at work I lost my mind. Think *The Wolf of Wall Street* again. I can't recall exactly what happened. My guess is that one of my employees let a sale slip through his fingers. As he explained the situation to me, I rose from my desk, berated him, and as he retreated from my presence, I hurled a stapler at him. The stapler smashed on the wall and broke into pieces. He scurried away, looking back over his shoulder at me in fear. Just another day in the office.

For a long time I was a Level 1 Positional Leader in the way I parented as well. My children would ask me, "Why do we have to do this?" My response would be, "Because I'm your dad, and I said so." This might be a small and silly example, but in even something like this you can see that I was using my *position* in their lives to garner respect, which I hoped would, at the very least, fear them into obedience. And, if they didn't do what I asked of them, I certainly wouldn't throw a stapler at them, but I would sometimes become angry.

Let's continue to break this down. When I hurled the stapler at my employee, what was going on beneath the surface? On one level, it's human and natural to experience conflict at work. Sometimes people get angry. And yes, sometimes a leader needs to put some pressure on the person they are leading in order to push them to a new level of discovering their gifts. On another level, however, throwing a stapler was reactive and completely different from an *organic*, constructive argument. I may have been frustrated with him, but my *rage* was connected to my own personal issues that I was yet to deal with. I scapegoated him. I used my position to justify bad behavior. What I did to him was hurtful and completely unnecessary. Can you relate? Maybe you know a boss who treats you like this. Maybe you have treated others like this.

I don't remember the person's name. I don't remember his face, either, though I'd probably recognize it if I ran into him at the store. There were dozens of other scenes in my early leadership days just like this. The first thing I'd say to him if our paths ever crossed would be something I should have said decades before: "I'm sorry." Maybe he wouldn't even remember the instance. Or maybe it was so scarring for him that he still thinks about it often. Either way, I would take responsibility for who I was during that time and how my actions sometimes left a path of destruction.

When leaders begin to move from Level 1 to Level 2, they begin apologizing and taking responsibility for their actions. In fact, when they apologize and acknowledge their mistakes, it sometimes *strengthens* the connection with those who they are leading. People can see that a leader is aware, authentic, and accountable. When we apologize, we are telling someone that *they* are important and that our relationship with them is important. The Eighth Step of recovery, which we'll explore in a moment, is about reconnecting us back to people and taking responsibilities for our actions. It won't be difficult for us to apologize when we make a mistake in leadership because we'll know we're in process toward reaching our potential. It won't be difficult to surround ourselves with others who see our blindspots because we know we can't lead on our own. Our acceptance and willingness to change sets a trajectory for others to follow, so that we're all transforming together and increasing our potential.

This brings us back to the Johari Window. Our arena is being massively authentic and real. People unaware of their blindspots might have a hard time apologizing because they don't think they've done anything wrong. When I worked for "Half a Car," a company which revolutionized the automobile industry with a new model for leasing, founder and CEO Eustace Wolfington always used to say that the two most important words in the English language are "I'm sorry." Another one I would add is "thank you."

Now, fast forward. In the middle of writing this book, my son, Nick, who is a broadcaster for the San Jose Sharks organization, called me and said, "Angie (his fiancée) and I talked, and we'd be honored if you would officiate our wedding." I definitely began tearing up.

Believe me, I've made countless mistakes in my life, but one thing I'm proud of is that I never gave up on my ability to be a good father. My kids had to heal in their own ways from their childhoods, which was fractured by divorce as well as the anger and discontent I brought into our family's household. But as I grew as a leader and as a father, with the 12 Steps forming my emotional intelligence, I never gave up on what my relationships with my kids could be. I took responsibility for my mistakes and gave them the space they needed to heal. I never stopped calling them and pursuing them. I never missed one of their sporting events. My son, Dax, once looked up into the stands during football practice for the community college where he played. I was the only fan there, in the middle of the workday. When he graduated, he told me, "Thank you for always being there." No matter where I lived I very seldom missed a game.

My faith helped take me from a positionally-motivated leader to a relationally-motivated leader in both the workplace and at home. It continues to form me today. That's why my relationships with my kids are better than ever before.

The Eighth Step of Celebrate Recovery reads, "We made a list of all the persons we had harmed and became willing to make amends to them all." In this step we're invited to acknowledge and evaluate the ripple effects from our mistakes. Who have we hurt on a deep level? What behavior led to this hurt? What role did our addictions or attachments have in our behavior? The exercise is to write down who we believe we've harmed. We're not trying to beat ourselves up here. The goal is not to keep score for every little thing we've done wrong. But rather, we want to honestly evaluate where we think we've hurt someone on a significant level.

This step also helps connect us back to one of the core reasons why we should be motivated to change: *for others*. To serve them better. To lead them better. To love them better. Isn't "self-development" an interesting term? Yes, we are personally transforming, but what is the point? Sure, we want to be healthier. We want to grow. We want to reach our max capacity. But again, why? The goal of all of this development is to overflow into the world around us. Our transformation isn't meant to be self-centered. Our transformation might entail a deep dive into our very selves as we evaluate who we are and what we've done, but the goal of that is to serve others better.

You can sometimes see this dynamic on display in personality tests. People become so intrigued with their personality traits that they neglect the point of going on this introspective journey in the first place. In gaining a better understanding of our personality, our gifts, our blindspots, and our tendencies, we bring more awareness into our *relationships*. As I've mentioned, since I now know that in stress I become a high "D" (Dominance) in the DISC I can be more aware of how I might seek to control people when I'm stressed. So, now, I can step back, take a deep breath, maybe even communicate with those around me about where I'm at emotionally, and seek to be more proactive—intentional and grounded in my next movements—rather than reactive (i.e. throwing a stapler).

You can sometimes unfortunately see this dynamic on display in religion, too. All the focus on a "personal relationship with Jesus" can make someone self-righteous and isolated in their own private faith, rather than more loving and selfless, as Jesus demonstrated.

Part of all this, I think, is our culture. Especially in America, we can be hyper-individualistic. As I write this a couple of years after a global pandemic, it seems like we as a society have become even more isolated and less community-focused. The political polarization in our society hasn't helped matters. Step 8 helps connects us back to what this whole journey of transformation is about. *Relationships*. This step moves us into being "willing to make amends to them all"—the people we have deeply harmed. In specifically naming how our actions have hurt people in the past, we grow in both self-awareness and relational-awareness. This goes back to our arena again. We re-orient our minds toward relationships. We gain an understanding of our own tendencies, as well as how others function in their own unique way and interact with our personality. We become more sensitive, more empathetic, more curious, and our perspective expands. We become less shackled by our past simply because we understand it. Instead of it holding us back, now it is propelling us forward to love and serve people more fully.

Understand this, folks: this is about reaching your max capacity and full potential. Understand your why. Doing this hard work of transformation is a massive *why* because as you change yourself, you will help change others. In his book on discovering your why, Simon Sinek goes deep with not only what you're trying to accomplish but why you're doing so. When we go deep with our why, that's where transformation happens.

My mom again comes to mind when I think of someone who was proactive in her leadership. When she was fifty-nine years old, she took over the family business in the wake of my dad passing away from alcoholism. My dad had, for some reason, cancelled their life insurance policy eight months before he passed away. I think he was trying to save anywhere he could because his company was struggling financially. Of course he had no idea he would soon have a stroke related to his drinking problems. The day he had a stroke, he went to work and the bank said the company was upside-down in their checking. He hadn't been paying enough attention to the cashflow of the company. Leaving at work every day at noon to go to the bar, he had no idea that someone in the mechanics department had been stealing automobile parts and throwing them out the backdoor for his buddy to pick up and resell.

With no life insurance policy, Mom had no choice but to figure out how to run the business if she wanted to make money for the family. She had to learn how to be a leader out of survival. She had no experience leading a business. She ran a household but had never been in a leadership position work-wise. And now all of a sudden she was overseeing a struggling business with a broken culture in a piece-of-crap building in the Middle of Nowhere, Ohio. The automobile and truck industry, especially when it came to dealerships, was mostly a "good old boys" club. Mom went back to school to learn business but did not tell her professors she was already running a business; nor did she tell her employees she was going to school at night.

Mom became a student of business, leadership, and a master of her emotions. She found out how to connect and lead these down-home country boys. She brought outcasts together. She found a business partner who she trusted. They weeded out the toxicity in the culture. She got rid of the business manager who had been there for twenty-five years and the manager in the "parts" department who knew of the theft that was going on. She drew a line in the sand, "Here's what we're doing, are you with me?" Eighty percent of her employees stayed and helped make the business into a thriving company once more. She and her partner looked at the past business failures and revolutionized the company. Through her career she expanded the company to three locations. At ninety years old, she sold it.

The more we learn from how we have failed as leaders, the more free we will be. The most miserable leaders I know are the ones who are afraid to confront how they have failed. This blindness usually creates a toxic culture where people with the most power aren't held accountable. Valuable feedback that could make the entire company better goes unheard because people's egos are fragile. Boy, isn't that the case of businesses whether they are small, medium, and large? *That* is a pandemic right there. You can take every leadership class in the world, but if you can't look in the mirror and get honest with yourself about your own shortcomings as a leader, you're in trouble.

I always used to take things personally whenever anyone would call me out on something I did. My anger would flare up. I'd grow defensive. I'd start keeping score. I'd try to win the argument, all based on insecurity. It became a binary, me vs. you conflict, in which I was determined to come out on top. Happen to know a boss like that? Someone brings up something that needs to be improved within the company and they're met with defensiveness?

Don't get me wrong, my ego still gets wounded sometimes, but now I see that feedback as useful information that helps me to become a better partner, friend, and husband. This is a "making amends" attitude. One could even incorporate this practice with our three questions to ask at the end of the day: *What did I do right today? What did I learn? What must I change?* Often times it's our relationships—and the tension and complexity that exist within them—that give us the best cues for what we need to change. As I've mentioned, even asking the question, "What's my role in this?" can change everything.

We are all accountable to each other because we are ultimately all connected to one another. As Brené Brown writes, "Staying vulnerable is a risk we have to take if we want to experience connection." If we are guarded, defensive, or unreceptive to feedback, then we aren't being vulnerable as leaders. People will feel like we don't care about them because we aren't connecting with them. In *Everyone Communicates Few Connect*, John Maxwell mentions in Chapter 10 that one of the best ways to connect with those who you are leading is acknowledging mistakes, apologizing, and making amends. Again, people don't want to follow someone who thinks they are always right; they want to follow someone who is relentlessly real.

Just about all of the 12 Steps can be traced back to humility and integrity. And when you open yourself up to be accountable to other people—besides yourself and God—what you're doing is adding another level of integrity. Leading with fear—throwing staplers—will lead to a culture of silence—suppressed frustration—where people feel more and more unheard because they are afraid to speak. They'll feel more disconnected from leadership. This can be at home *and* the workplace, right? Ever see your kids disconnect? You might want to look in the mirror.

A culture of fear, paradoxically, will likely make people not work as hard at a company because they won't trust its trajectory. People will feel discontent and unfulfilled, and leadership, as a consequence, won't ever get the chance to move to Level 2 (which is rooted in relationship) or Level 3 (where rich connectedness leads to purpose and fulfillment). If you as a leader don't like what's going on *out* there, ask yourself, "What is my role in this?"

One time I was asked by leadership at a restaurant to be their coach. After assessing the culture of the restaurant, they asked where they could improve. I told them that they needed to communicate better. They disagreed. Eight months later, the relationship between the owners and employees fell apart. Communication, even if it's painful, is usually the place we have to start. Usually the first signs of a problem come down to communication in some way.

Have you ever played golf? Depending on the time of day you play, the sun might cast your shadow across the green, and you'll have to make sure that it's not extending into the putting line of your playing partner. This is because it's more difficult to decipher which way the green is breaking if you are blocking the person's line with your shadow. If you comfortably stood there, blocking someone's line with your shadow, it's likely you'd be asked to move. If it happened a couple times, you'd probably be perceived as someone who is very unaware.

Leadership is like this, I think. We all cast a shadow, and it probably extends in different lengths and directions depending on the circumstance. What makes up the shadow? It might be your blindspots, tendencies, or insecurities. It might be past mistakes or lies that you tell yourself. Not one of us is free from having a shadow. But as leaders, the spotlight is on us more. In other words, more people will *notice* our shadows. And our shadows have the ability to negatively affect someone else's vision. People might think they aren't leaders, but they are parents; they are siblings; they are friends. Well, then you're a leader. We're designed to be relational and therefore we are all meant to be leaders.

As leaders we must be humbly aware of our shadows, and we must be *willing to make amends* whenever our shadows get in the way. When we do this we let people know that we are in their corner and that we care about their success. We also model for them humility and introspection so that they can feel comfortable to go on a journey of change as well. Why would someone ever consider the journey of change in a culture where they feel pressured to be perfect? Change comes with mistakes.

I'll close this chapter by listing some of the principles in the mastermind course I teach based on Maxwell's *Everyone Communicates Few Connect*. I hope these principles serve as a benediction for you today in any area of your life when you have been entrusted to lead.

- *Connectors own their mistakes.*
- *They are willing to make amends.*
- *They increase their influence in every situation, even the difficult situations where they are wrong.*
- *Connectors are all about others.*
- *They realize connecting goes beyond words and that it requires lots of energy.*
- *Connectors inspire people.*
- *Connectors live what they communicate.*
- *Connectors are relational leaders.*

How are you communicating? How are you connecting? As leaders we sometimes think that we have to have it all together in order to be a good leader. But it's actually our willingness to be vulnerable and to be held accountable that makes good leaders. Relationships animate our change. If we really, *really* want to have great relationships, we have to have clarity in our own self so that we can be all we need to be for others. Why do we want to have great relationships? If we know why, we have to be massively clear in our own growth. Once we're massively clear in our own growth, we can serve as a conduit to help and serve others.

Scan the QR code to watch a special message from Bart about Chapter Eight.

CHAPTER 9
FREEDOM THROUGH FORGIVENESS

When I first started working the Steps, I hit a wall at Step 8—making a list of those I had harmed—and Step 9—making direct amends. These are the "forgiveness steps." I never made a list of people who were hurt by my addiction. I never reached out to apologize to people who were hurt by my addiction. I had humility in the sense that I admitted I needed help and leaned on God each morning for help. But I was yet to discover what I would call "relational humility," which Steps 8 and 9 guide us toward. I was accountable to God and my sponsor and myself for my sobriety, but I was yet to become accountable to *others* for my character defects; for my actions; for how I had harmed others.

In other words, I didn't really keep myself accountable for my actions, just as my parents didn't keep me accountable growing up. That's also probably why I chose the person that I did for my first or second sponsor upon graduating from the Adrian Center: he didn't really keep me accountable either. And I liked it that way, or, subconsciously, didn't know better. Yes, I stayed sober. Yes, in that sense, there was accountability. But I never took the Steps deeper than that. My introspection began and ended with the binary question: Am I avoiding alcohol and drugs? For thirty-seven years (and counting) I'm proud to say that the answer has been "yes." But what about behavior? What about the effects of my past behavior? What about the people's lives who were impacted by my character defects? By my addiction to drugs and alcohol? By my addiction to attention and affection?

Venturing deeper into faith is what ultimately led me to the door of Celebrate Recovery. There was a Celebrate Recovery group at the church I was going to, and that's when the Steps began to take on new form for me. I went to AA meetings for years but I always felt like there was something missing when we talked about a "higher power." When CR talked about the higher power being Jesus Christ, that really connected for me in that particular season of my life. Much of what is in this book, especially the second half of this book, comes from how CR helped me to take the Steps deeper in my life. As I've mentioned, anyone who works the steps over and over will see them come to life in different ways.

I've said this before, but if you're doing a deep dive into the steps, I can't recommend enough that you do that alongside a sponsor. You might decide that you even want to consult a therapist. I not only had a sponsor but have gone to counseling in some shape or form the last thirty-seven years. That was a big piece for me in going deeper.

But it was fitting nonetheless for Step 8 and Step 9 to take more form for me as I ventured deeper into my faith. That's what faith, at its best, should do. In connecting deeper with God, faith should also help you to connect more beautifully to the world around you: to those you love, to those you're leading, to strangers, to your true self, to creation. As humans, we are relational beings. How have we forgotten this truth? A healthy, committed faith should inspire you to cultivate genuine connection in your relationships.

In CR, the humility and accountability that began in Alcoholics Anonymous at the Adrian Center ten years before was taken to a deeper level. There was a new level of commitment at this point. When I walked into that room in front of a group of men and had to get deeper about my insecurity, anger, and narcissism, it really forced me to work the steps at a deeper level. For perhaps the first time in my life, as crazy as that sounds, I made myself accountable to others. I began to see the ripple effects of my character defects and desired to change, not just because my buddy had gotten sober and looked great (one of the reasons I checked into the Adrian Center), not just because I felt empty and miserable, but because of how my actions left a very real impact, whether positive or negative, on others. I attended church, Bible study, and Celebrate Recovery, no longer because of the Mercedes Benzes in the parking lot, no longer because of prosperity and my obsession with success, but because of the change I could see unfolding not only in myself but also in my relationships. This was taken to a whole new level in the eighth and ninth steps of Celebrate Recovery. I made my list. I reached out to others who I had harmed. I sought "do to others as you would have them do to you" (Luke 6:31). In my home. In the workplace. In the world. In *life*.

❖❖❖

The ninth step of Celebrate Recovery reads, "We made direct amends to such people (the ones on our list) whenever possible, except when to do so would injure them to others."

These relationally-focused steps can indeed be heavy. It's not easy to confront the wreckage of our past life. It's not easy to consider what role we had in hurting someone else. You could be in the workplace or your home, and this same dynamic might be on display. If perception is reality, then the way others perceive our actions is, in some way or another, valuable data for how we are leading. In this step it can seem like we are merely swimming in negativity, relentlessly venturing deeper into the negative impact of our actions. But that's not the point. It's not about dwelling on our mistakes from the day before or decade before; it's about realizing when we were villains in someone's story for a particular moment in time. These steps still aren't sounding more fun, are they? Our making amends, actually, as long as we are centered in our identity as loved and accepted, leads to liberation. That's right, *liberation*. I love the quote by Tony Robbins, "Our past does not equal our future." The point isn't to relive the past. It's to help someone else's heart to heal. It's not about us; it's about *them*.

In making a list of all the people we harmed, in making direct amends whenever appropriate, we are fully confronting our darkness by naming how our actions wounded others. As 1 John 1:9 says, "If we confess our sins, he is faithful and just and will forgive us our sins and purify us from all unrighteousness." I've heard Christians before say that God can't forgive us if we haven't asked Him for forgiveness. I'm not sure I agree with that. As a believer, I trust Christ covered our sinfulness and brokenness by dying on the cross. But I do understand the sentiment. In naming how we have hurt others, in confessing these relational sins, we open ourselves up to receive forgiveness from God, and thus, we too must forgive ourselves. If we can't forgive ourselves then do we really believe in God's forgiveness?

A lot of people struggle to get sober, in my opinion, because their negative self-view is directly related to their broken relationships. That's understandable. *Nothing* pains me more than considering how I have hurt the people in my life I love the most. Even thinking back to the "stapler guy" I discussed last chapter breaks my heart. When I revisit my past life, I can't believe the person I used to be. But maybe the fact I can write about it reveals I no longer feel shame for the past. God has forgiven me for my outburst that morning at the dealership, and therefore I need to forgive myself.

The freedom of forgiveness is not always found in someone else's forgiveness of us. Sometimes we can't locate that person to make direct amends. Other times we'll find that a person isn't ready to forgive and in fact might never be ready to forgive. But humbly asking for forgiveness can help us to *move on*, learn from our mistakes, and take what we've learned into serving and leading people better. We surrender our lists to God. We seek forgiveness directly with those on our list when appropriate. When we allow God to forgive us and follow His lead by forgiving ourselves, we are trusting that our past mistakes have no bearing on our future. Our mistakes can only strengthen how we lead people today. Why? Because of how we've chosen to learn from those mistakes.

So, how do we decide if we should reach out to someone directly and ask for forgiveness? Consider the caveat: "except when to do so would injure them or others." I once attended a Christian conference that was focused on sexual integrity. In one of the sessions the speaker recommended that we spend the remainder of the afternoon calling our significant other and sharing with them the exact nature of all our sexual sins throughout the entirety of our lives. As you might imagine, this was a recipe for disaster. It made many loved ones feel insecure, angry, and threatened. Don't get me wrong: honesty with your significant other is paramount. It's the key ingredient to a healthy, long-lasting relationship. But we should also long to protect one another's hearts and use discretion according to our own unique relationship with any particular person. I once met someone who told me that he would call his wife immediately every time that he lusted. I can't imagine this made his wife feel very confident. A wise man once told me that your significant other shouldn't be your accountability partner. Yes, you need to tell someone. Yes, you need to be honest with your spouse. Yes, you need to confess to your spouse unfaithfulness and be transparent about your struggles and flaws. But we should also seek to protect one another's hearts. Be careful about throwing the cigarette out the window because you're realizing you shouldn't smoke anymore. You might start a forest fire. Be careful about data dumping just to make yourself feel better.

Again, the goal of this step is liberation. Let's take a moment to consider the real effects of true liberation: to be free, to have peace, to be able to breathe, to not have a knot in our stomach, to stand up straighter and be a little more authentic. Can you taste it yet? Can you sense the freedom that is within reach for you as you change? Remember, we can't be honest if we don't start with ourselves. Honesty starts with self-integrity. If we're not honest with ourselves, we're not going to be honest with others. When we're honest, we walk lighter; we have more peace.

Liberation is not scapegoating. It's not cheaply alleviating guilt. It's not a bandaid. This step is about directly naming the conviction you feel while *also* meeting people where they are. Some people will feel validated that you named the pain you caused in their lives. Others will be upset and even re-triggered to see your name pop up on their phone. Our apologies, if they are genuine, have to be tailored for the person's personality in the context of the pain. Sometimes that might mean *not* making direct contact yet making amends through God and with yourself nonetheless. It might mean writing them a letter. Making amends is *about* them, but it's *for* you; to help heal their heart but also liberate ourselves so we can be a better person on the other side of this. This is big. You are only as sick as your secrets. Maybe it's wise to not make direct amends, but you need to talk about it with someone, preferably a therapist. *Someone* has to know. If we don't do this step, we're more tempted to feel shame, which causes us to return to our hurts, habits, or hangups, which starts the addiction cycle all over again (see image on next page). We want to get to the other side to create new patterns. Doing this puts it in the past.

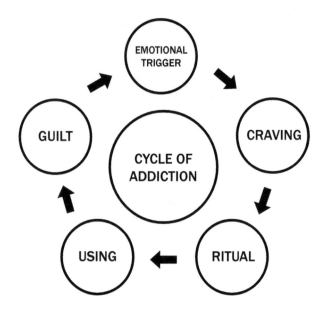

Starting to see how complex this is and how self-aware we must be? Even if someone says they forgive you, they might not trust your apology because they still don't feel like you understood their pain. We can tell if our making direct amends is genuine or not by how our faith is paired with action. Remember, people are right to be skeptical about an addict's apology. Many addicts can BS their way through anything. All their lives, they have manipulated, lied, cheated, and stole to get what they want. As we grow, however, we're animated by honesty, curiosity, humility, and soul-searching. This step requires so much discretion, and, through it all, we must trust that even if we decide that personally making amends would cause harm or injury, that God forgives us. Again, use your sponsor or therapist as a guide.

Think of this step like getting on the ground and placing an empty pail beneath a spigot. We've taken our emptiness—our wrongdoings, our flaws, the wounds we've caused others—and we've humbly bended our knees beneath the spigot. We're unafraid to get messy, to dirty up our knees and legs and feet. It is up to God, then, as well as others, to fill our empty pale. If our seeking of forgiveness is genuine, God will *always* fill our pail with His love and grace even when others aren't ready to forgive. But here's the tough part if you're someone who tends to beat yourself up or have a negative self-view. When our pail is filled up, what do we do? Do we remain on the ground and dump out the pail, unable to accept that we are truly forgiven? Or do we accept and receive this gift of love and grace, rise to our feet, and use the water in our pail as nourishment for others? We can't transform if we aren't moving forward. It's really the only way, or else we'll get caught in a loop and define ourselves by all the mistakes we made in the past.

Step 9 in Celebrate Recovery's *Stepping Out of Denial into God's Grace* (which is all of our journeys, right?) is accompanied by the simple subtitle: "GRACE." The verse it gives is Matthew 5:23-24: "Therefore, if you are offering your gift at the altar and there remember that your brother or sister has something against you, leave your gift there in front of the altar. First go and be reconciled to them; then come and offer your gift." Be careful what you do because you are going to have to tell someone about it. In Step 9, the acrostic for GRACE is:

God's gift
Receive by our faith
Accepted by God's love
Christ paid the price
Everlasting gift

Not accepting God's love and grace is selfish and egocentric. That's what unforgiveness is at the core, right? It's EGO—*Edging God Out*. We fool ourselves into thinking that our perception of ourselves is more accurate than God's. We fool ourselves into thinking that we are paying for our sins by remaining defeated on the ground. That's not humility. And so, we remain on the ground, unable to move on with our lives, wasting water and going nowhere. If we've truly gotten to that place of emptiness, humbly positioning ourselves to be filled by God's love and grace, then I think we can come to a certain closure with our pain. The love and grace we've received eventually overflows onto others. Grace always animates.

The point of Celebrate Recovery, of confession, of accountability, is not to dwell upon your sin. It took me a while to learn that. It's *movement*. In Step 8 and Step 9, we are in movement toward confronting the impact of our wrongdoing relationally, but in doing that we are also in movement toward closure.

Whereas there are times when making direct amends might cause harm or injury to others, when it comes to leadership, I would argue that making amends is almost *always* necessary. We should make amends "whenever possible," as the ninth step says. This is important because tension festers. It multiplies itself like bacteria. Consider this scenario…

A CEO is sitting in his office. He's having a stressful day, experiencing the relentless pressure of the board for the company to hit their third quarter numbers. The CEO knows that if they don't hit these numbers, serious changes are on the horizon. The CEO hears a knock on his door. It's one of his most dedicated managers. The manager brings up something minor—something that isn't on the CEO's radar on this particularly stressful day—and snaps at the manager, pressuring him and his team to make more sales. Have you had this happen before? The stress and pressure keeps getting projected downward. Tension might not only fester between the CEO and the manager but also the manager and his team. However, *if* the CEO had the self-awareness to get introspective about the interaction, he might intentionally seek out the manager a few minutes later and say, "Listen, I didn't like the way I talked to you back there. I'm just under a lot of stress today from the board, and I took that out on you. I'm sorry. Let's do the best we can this quarter, together, as a team." In just a few humble seconds, the CEO has extinguished the tension, strengthened his relationship with his manager, and maybe even empowered his manager to lead with a similar introspection and humility.

There are three pieces that are so important to making amends: *communication*, *expectations*, and *acceptance*. Life is all about communication, but we're almost being formed in our society (and certainly during the pandemic) not to communicate with anyone. If you're in recovery, you have to be able to communicate, especially when you're hurting. Expectations and acceptance are directly related because the higher the expectations, the higher acceptance has to be.

Why are we afraid to ask co-workers or teammates for forgiveness? Simple: insecurity. Our insecurities are aspects of ourselves that we don't want others to see or experience and, thus, we spend a lot of energy trying to hide them. In the Johari window, it's our facades, our masks. Somehow we think that if we admit we're wrong, we'll be respected less. The truth is that we'll likely be respected *more* in our vulnerability. We'll be *more* trusted, *more* approachable. Once again, people want *real*, not *right*.

If we can get to that steady place of fully accepting ourselves—as people who are loved, in process, and have many more lessons to learn—then we'll spend less energy trying to mask and protect our insecurities. We will have *more* energy to *connect* with others. Jesus loves us and forgives us, so why would we not love and forgive ourselves? When we waste energy masking our insecurities, do we really think we're fooling those who are following us? We've all had bosses who have projected their own insecurities on others, who we can tell are miserable to the core, and we've all lost respect for those bosses. When we can do the hard inner work to gain acceptance for ourselves—for our journeys, for our personalities, for our blindspots—it frees us up to be transparent and apologize more. Our egos aren't threatened anymore. We know we're going to forgive ourselves, so why would we *not* ask others for forgiveness when we know we've hurt them?

Now, again, discretion is key with this step. In leadership, there is such a thing as over-sharing that can lead to a loss of respect. Maybe this is an absurd example, but being transparent with a worker about "almost firing them" or, if you're a coach, with a student-athlete about "almost cutting them," will likely just sow seeds of insecurity within *them*. That's not honest and transparent; that's just mean.

It's all about motive. Why are we sharing what we're sharing? Are we feeling insecure and masking those insecurities with "authenticity," for example, apologizing for something ridiculous because we're desperate for a compliment? If we're good leaders, then we are committed to introspection. It's human to have insecurities, but we must ask ourselves: Who is standing in the crossfire of our insecurities?

One "formula" I've found to be helpful making amends with people I'm leading is being both quick and direct.

"Hey, Jack, I didn't like my tone back there. I'm sorry."

Move on.

"Hey, Jill, I didn't do a good job of listening to your feedback about the company vision in our team meeting. I'm sorry. I'd like to send an email out to the team expressing the different aspects of your vision."

Move on.

Some "making amends," say, if it was a really intense argument, may require going out to lunch and "hashing out" grievances. But most apologies, I've found, ought to be quick and to the point. An intense apology for a minor slip could make an employee feel uneasy. The person might think to themselves, *Why does my boss overthink and obsess over every little interaction?*

And, once again, employees can tell if apologies are genuine. If we're apologizing every single week to our employees for raising our voice or losing our patience, we're showing employees that cheap apologies are more important than actually changing. Yes, our same tendencies will likely resurface, but when we do the inner work to keep the change, our apologies are more genuine and mean all the more. And eventually the behavior will go away.

The opportunity is that leadership exposes our insecurities. Our insecurities are more difficult to mask because they directly affect others. We all know when we've dropped the ball. Humility helps us look for signs of our insecurities: our opportunities to grow and become more compassionate, holistic leaders. Blame, defensiveness, ego inflation, anger, or lack of listening are all signals for growth—for where we need to do the inner work to narrow our facades.

In Step 9 we are reminded of our connectedness with one another. We are accountable to one another for our actions. We are trying to create a culture *together*. A culture that is healthy, fun, and purposeful, whether it's at home or in the workplace. A culture rooted in selfless service and excellence, whether you're a leader or a follower. Not everyone has to be best friends, but disconnectedness often festers and makes cultures less, enjoyable, efficient, and accountable. Gossip, backstabbing, or stubbornness might all be signs of disconnectedness. And, as we said earlier, disconnectedness leads to lousy communication. And lousy communication leads to broken homes and companies.

I learned from John Maxwell that culture forms around core values. Making amends has to rank high in core values, in my opinion, because that's the primary means for repairing disconnectedness. Making amends allows humility to flourish. Making amends is often a route for meaningful conversations. Making amends paves the way for honest, rich relationships to form. Making amends is how we let one another know that we care about each other.

Scan the QR code to watch a special message from Bart about Chapter Nine.

CHAPTER 10
CABIN IN THE WOODS

The wind howled through the cracks in the wall. I sat in a little rocking chair in front of the fireplace, trying to stay warm. I thought about taking a hot bath, but the tub had to have been designed for a smurf, not a grown man who was six foot two. I had no Internet, no phone, no television, no electronics whatsoever. The cabin was desolate, five hundred square feet, smack-dab in the woods. All I had was a lamp, a stove, a journal, a pen, and my Bible. This tiny cabin would be my home for the next thirty days.

Why would I go to a cabin in the woods for a month? Well, I was in a broken relationship and really wanted to fix it. My therapist, Bryan, sensed some patterns I kept bringing into relationships. Those patterns needed to be interrupted. I had been to Bryan for probably three months and consistently had issues that were going on with flirtation and anger. I really wanted to figure out, between the divorce and this relationship, what was going on within me that this kind of destruction kept happening. My therapist could see that I was blocked. He kept telling me the same thing, but I kept doing the same behavior. I always had a reason to blame my mom or my dad or my relationships. I was angry all the time, not at all liking who I was, so of course I had to put it on someone else. I was in a rut.

"You need intensive," Bryan said to me one day.

"Intensive?" I said.

"Thirty days in a cabin, just you, your Bible, and a journal."

Because my relationships had been so disastrous and I was desperate to change the narrative, I said yes. For thirty days, I would meet with my therapist, Bryan, at eight o'clock in the morning for an hour, and then I would return to the cabin for the next twenty-three hours. This was where Celebrate Recovery and my growing Christian faith had taken me: deeper into the abyss, and, thus, the truth. Sounds fun, huh?

Faith is like that sometimes, most of the time. It's not always emotional highs during praise and worship on Sunday. It's not always walking out of the sanctuary "feeling good" about oneself. It's not about prosperity. It's not Pollyanna. If that's all faith is to someone—a positive boost—then they are likely missing out on its transforming nature. Faith is messy and real and, at times, excruciating. My insecurities had me feel like I had an evil serpent coiled around me at all times. Thirty intensive days in the cabin—hanging out with someone who wasn't my best friend (me)— like recovery, was meant to chop off the serpent's head. What do I mean exactly? I had a haunting dream in the cabin where there was a serpent laying next to me. I sensed that my job was to find out where the serpent started so I could eradicate it. I had to find the beginning of that thing and get rid of it forever. In other words, there is the behavior—which could be drinking or sexual integrity or anger—but there is a *reason* for the behavior. What I learned in the cabin is that you have to find the root, the beginning of the serpent. Until you find the head and cut it off, the same behaviors will keep popping up. It's kind of like a garden. If you just pull up the dandelions but don't pull up the weeds, they will keep coming back. Spiritual disciplines like prayer, journaling, therapy, confiding in a sponsor, etc. all help us to find the serpent's head and cut it off.

In the cabin, Bryan wanted me to be alone with God and disconnected from everyone who I could blame. I had already made amends to so many other people, but now it was time to make amends with myself. To look in the mirror and say, "Bart, I forgive you."

In John Comer's *The Ruthless Elimination of Hurry,* he talks about the power of stopping, learning to be quiet, and listening to God and yourself. But here's the kicker: you have to be okay hanging out with yourself. After meeting with Bryan the first morning, I went back to the cabin and spent the day reading through the New Testament. Then, I wrote a long, ten-page letter to my mother.

I read it to Bryan the next morning, and he simply said, "Great, go back and do it again."

I read through the New Testament and wrote another ten-page letter to Mom.

"Great," he said again, "go back and do it again."

I wrote about my mother and read the New Testament each day for over a week.

At first the letters were laden with grief and even anger. I was grateful for how present she was in my life, unlike my father, but felt like she never held me accountable. I felt like I had a broken moral framework from the start and no solid grounding. Pretty crazy to blame someone else, huh? It was a breakthrough for me to realize that this was why I felt neglected, though I wasn't. I just never seemed to develop much of a conscience because I never faced consequences for my actions. By the end of the week, the letters were grace-filled, thanking her for the lessons she *did* teach me and how her love for me strengthened my love for my own children. But it didn't start that way. It started with *blame, blame, blame*. The ambivalence was guiding me toward areas in which I needed to change: opportunities for transformation. I gained more grace for myself, rather than judging my journey, but could also see that, just like my strict boundaries with alcohol and drugs, I now had to develop a strict moral code in other areas of my life. In his book *Just Like Jesus*, Max Lucado talks about having a heart transplant, meaning that we need to install Jesus's heart within ourselves. I started getting a new set of glasses. I was learning to love me. In doing that, I realized it wasn't about those other people I had been blaming. After the cabin, my mom and I became best friends.

Something else jumped out at me during that first week. After those first couple of days in the cabin, I learned that I didn't want to hang out with myself because I didn't like myself. But as I read through the New Testament every day, my heart was stirred to read that 310 times Scripture said that we were loved by God. This really started to sink in. For the first time in my life, I was beginning to realize I was loved unconditionally. Instead of writing down all the things I didn't like about myself, as I had proverbially done my entire life, my heart was slowly opened to accepting and embracing who God made me to be.

Finally, on the ninth day, Bryan said, "Great, now go write about your dad." My dad was there physically but not emotionally. He was a car dealer who wanted to drink with his buddies and hang out on his boats. One day I remember picking him up at the airport. I took his luggage, and we walked by a few screaming kids. "Don't have those," he said. *Uh, hello?* I thought to myself. *I was one of those!* I obviously had a lot to process, and for ten days, I wrote about Dad. In the cabin I learned to forgive him for how distant he was as a father; to love him for who he was as a person; and to cherish the memories we made together later in his life when we actually became very close.

Next, Bryan said to me, "Great, now go write about your brother." For a little less than a week, I wrote letters to my brother. I was jealous of my brother. I had always been jealous of my brother. But the more I learned to love myself, the less I was jealous of him. I was beginning to see how my past affected some of my tendencies but how I needed to deal with some of those tendencies directly if I wanted to one day have a happy, committed marriage. Without those thirty days in the woods, I don't know if I'd be nearing a decade of marriage with the love of my life, Mary, today.

Lastly, in the final week, Bryan said, "Great, now go write a letter to yourself." What role did I play in loving myself? What role did I play in accepting myself? In that letter I took everything I had learned that month and wrote a loving—yes, *loving*—letter to myself. I couldn't be good enough for anybody else until God was enough for me, until *I* was enough for me. I had to give myself grace; only then could I give others grace. I was beginning to see myself the way God saw me.

Did those thirty days in the woods fix everything? No. In fact, remember that relationship I told you that I was trying to fix? Right when I got back home from the cabin, we had a fight, split up, and never got back together again. But those thirty days in the cabin taught me how to befriend myself; to learn to live life on life's terms, meaning to accept my own circumstances; and to love myself.

The tenth step of Celebrate Recovery says, "We continued to take personal inventory and when we were wrong, promptly admitted it." As 1 Corinthians 10:12 warns, "So, if you think you are standing firm, be careful that you don't fall!"

Now that we've worked through the majority of the steps and developed tools for introspection and making amends in our relationships, we are truly equipped for a "deep dive," whatever that might mean to you. There's no way I could have done my thirty-day retreat in the woods had I not developed the skills I learned from the Adrian Center, Celebrate Recovery, and from my growing faith. Had I attempted that twenty years before, I likely would have gone insane in the cabin. I would have been slashing at the walls or howling at the moon. I simply wouldn't have had the skills. The Steps are so brilliant because not only do they build on one another, but each one can also be taken deeper and deeper.

You might not need thirty days in a cabin, but I would encourage you to do something that breaks the everyday patterns of your life. That might be a three-day silent retreat at a monastery or a week-long yoga retreat with friends or even a simple weekend around the house without technology, where your down time is geared toward reading and journaling. Each of us can confidently journey inward—into places we have never gone before—with the assurance that Christ, the "hope of glory," is with us and in us (Colossians 1:27). This unshakable foundation is vital to remember whenever shame shows its face. No matter the ugliness we uncover, our relationship with God is never compromised. It is only forgotten sometimes on our end, but never on God's end.

Another way to think of Step 10 is *maintenance* for Step 8 and Step 9. As we make amends there will be some relationships where we must accept God's forgiveness, forgive ourselves, and move on, knowing we might not ever say "sorry" face-to-face to the person we wounded. Other apologies, however, will need to be made to maintain relationships that we still desire to flourish today. Relationships require *maintenance*, especially whenever we've caused significant wounding in the past. My thirty-day retreat in the woods was aimed toward my struggle in romantic relationships, with the hope of fixing the one I was in at the time. That didn't happen. It doesn't always work out that way. Our three questions can just as easily be applied to relationships as well: What did I do right? What did I learn? What must I change? Another question that has radically changed my life is: What's my role in this?

Under the guidance of a therapist (which I would again recommend confiding in as you practice this step), I was finally able to get to the origin of some of my patterns. Awareness helped me to understand what was going on in my mind and then establish positive habits that would help me to change my behavior. I wouldn't meet Mary for almost another decade, but those thirty days in the woods equipped me to one day be the best husband I could be.

Maintenance can, again, feel bent toward negativity, like there is always something wrong and you need to be on top of it. Remember, if you're beating yourself up, that's narcissistic. Keeping the change isn't about you. Maintenance is actually a positive opportunity to continually connect. How much more purpose do you experience with others when you know each other on a deep level? How can I serve my loved ones on the deepest level possible? How can I make someone feel as valued as possible?

Unfortunately in our age, we don't always value other people's opinions, and we often look for what is wrong instead of what is right. This step has little to do with pointing the finger at another person. It goes back to knowing *our* role and how you can serve people and help them to feel more valued.

In John 15:13, Jesus said, "There is no greater love than to lay down one's life for one's friends." Jesus said these words the evening before he would go to the cross to do that very thing. How does one get to such a selfless place of love?

Jesus had his own intensive therapy experience when he spent forty days in the desert (which Bryan modeled his intensive therapy after) and was tempted in every way, as he proved that he was who God made him to be. The devil tried to gain a foothold on Jesus's ego any way he could, just as that "serpent" did in the cabin with me, but Jesus did not budge. The devil's temptations revolved around trying to get Jesus to be more self-centered, to make the same mistake as Adam and Eve rather than humbly submitting to God's powerful plan for his life. Some pastors suggest that Jesus wasn't fully prepared for ministry until after that experience. I was not prepared for life until after the cabin.

Jesus modeled humility and obedience throughout his ministry. He was curious about people's deepest needs. He was radically present with others and almost always chose people over tasks. He was emotional, open, and honest. On the night before he died, he washed the feet of his disciples. The next day he would model the greatest love that has ever been shown. These were two incredible acts of servitude. Washing feet is profound in itself, but dying on the cross was the ultimate act of service and humility.

Maybe our purpose has yet to unfold because we haven't gone into the desert. Maybe we, too, need to confront our darkness head-on. Maybe we need to cut the heads off the serpents that entangle us. Maybe we need to draw a line in the sand with our demons. Maybe God is waiting for us to take the next step in embodying our potential. Go out into the desert, my friends. Go out into the woods.

The last chapter in John Maxwell's *Everyone Communicates Few Connect* is titled, "Connectors Live What they Communicate." Living what we communicate is one of the most difficult things about leadership. It happens through careful maintenance of our inner lives (like continually working to narrow our facades and blindspots in the Johari window) as well as attentive maintenance to our outer lives (our relationships). As Maxwell writes, "Credibility is the currency for leadership and communicators. With it they are solvent; without it they are bankrupt."

We get credible by getting consistent. When I graduated from the Adrian Center and embarked on a new way of life, I'm sure a lot of my friends were doubtful I had really changed. Heck, *I* was doubtful. After all, merely one month before I was a fixture at what-had-to-be some of the most raucous, reckless parties in San Jose. I was doing lines and drinking six-packs at work after all. Was I *really* going to stop cold turkey? I caught some flak from my buddies at the beginning, people who missed the "old Bart," but eventually they saw that I wasn't going back; that I truly hated my previous life; that I was determined to be sober. My discipline earned a certain level of respect. My commitment to my lifestyle said something about my dependability. Before, I didn't believe in anything so I fell for everything. Now I had a belief in something and refused to waiver.

The same dynamic was on display when I began to become more committed to my Christian faith. When I started attending church every Sunday, reading the Bible throughout the week, going to Celebrate Recovery, listening to Christian music, clearing out weekends for Christian retreats, etc., I'm sure there were some friends and family who were baffled by this new "Jesus Freak" that I was becoming. I'm sure many thought that my faith would just be a euphoric phase, soon to wear off, as it unfortunately is for some. It never did. I kept going deeper into my faith over the decades and continue to do so today.

Many of the closest people in my life aren't Christian and disagree with my beliefs, but they respect my faith because of its consistency. Because of how they can see it inspiring me to become a more loving and selfless person. I might be the only reflection of Jesus they ever see.

I'll say this about most addicts: one of our strengths is that we go *all-in* on what is important to us. The battle, often times, is directing our focus toward what is *really* important, healthy, and true. The only way to become consistent leaders is to change our mindsets from our old ways and root ourselves in the values we've uncovered.

A mindset rooted in the right things, day after day, will produce consistent selflessness, service, and strengthening others. Just as Steps 8 and 9 help us to move to a Level 2 leader who is anchored in the importance of relationships, it's consistency and discipline that, over time, help us to evolve to the next levels of leadership: Production, People Development, and Pinnacle. Level 3 extends beyond relationship and moves into production: effectiveness and efficiency. Maxwell says that the third level is the turning point when leaders become "change agents"—when their connection with those who they are leading overflows into purposeful work that changes their communities or world. Level 4, Maxwell says, can be summarized in the word "reproduction"—it's when there is such a strong culture that people grow to *become* leaders themselves. There is an intentional investment in personal development, as new leaders carry the mission into the future. And lastly, Level 5, Pinnacle, is where leaders "transcend their position, their organization, and sometimes their industry." They invest themselves in others' lives and leave a legacy.

There's a book called *Halftime* by Bob Buford that I quote all the time. Bob was a believer who owned several radio stations in Texas. His son, at twenty four years old, tragically drowned. Bob writes in his book that this tragedy changed everything. In his overbearing grief, he went from pursuing success to pursuing significance. Where am I going with this? Sometimes I think I want planes, trains, and automobiles, but when I listen to God, I get away from that. Tim Schurrer's book, *The Secret Society of Success*, is all about helping one person. It's about giving it away. It's about significance. Halftime doesn't just mean you're halfway through your life; it's when you decide that your life isn't about the world's definition of success anymore.

In AA and Recovery, they say that you can't keep what you don't give away. And that's exactly what Level 4 is about. You can't keep your sobriety if you don't help others stay sober.

The core meaning behind the title of this book is revealed in this chapter. *Keep the Change*. "Keep" means to "have or retain possession of." We keep the change by maintaining a lifestyle of steady growth (i.e. change). Change in this regard might begin with some pretty radical shifts, like checking into a recovery center. But then, throughout the rest of our lives, we change by rooting deeper and deeper into our values; by cultivating discipline and consistency. And therein lies the paradox. Our consistency as leaders *is* revealed *through* gradual change as we awaken more and more to the high-character, service-centered leader we are meant to be. The change I'm talking about is not switching leadership styles every other week. It's not creating a new vision every month. It's not implementing a new scheme for wealth accumulation every quarter. The change I'm talking about is a steady trajectory of becoming a better servant leader; of awakening more and more to our potential as we root ourselves in our values.

Yes, we will make mistakes on that journey. Plenty of them. But because we're in a state of continual maintenance, trying to cultivate awareness, we can, as Step 10 suggests, promptly admit when we are wrong. Admit. Learn. Move on. Change your mindset based on what you learned and change the world. True success—true significance—is all about connecting with others.

Scan the QR code to watch a special message from Bart about Chapter Ten.

CHAPTER 11

LEARNING TO KNOW

The first thing that I do every morning is get on my knees beside my bed and pray the Third Step prayer from Alcoholics Anonymous: "God, I offer myself to Thee—to build with me and to do with me as Thou wilt. Relieve me of the bondage of self, that I may better do Thy will. Take away my difficulties, that victory over them may bear witness to those I would help of Thy Power, Thy Love, and Thy Way of life. May I do Thy will always!"

After that, I pause, consider the words I just prayed, and then move on to the Seventh Step Prayer: "My Creator, I am now willing that you should have all of me, good and bad. I pray that you now remove from me every single defect of character which stands in the way of my usefulness to you and my fellows. Grant me strength, as I go out from here, to do your bidding. Amen."

This routine began nearly forty years ago when I graduated from the Adrian Center and was told to keep clinging to the Steps and to continue praying. I hardly knew what prayer was. I had very little semblance of a faith. Still, the prayers helped. Each day, the Third Step prayer helped anchor my heart in humility. Being on my *knees* anchored my heart in humility. It reminded me of my powerlessness (Step 1), in a belief in something outside of myself (Step 2), and the decision I had to make again, on that very day, to turn my addiction over to God (Step 3). The Seventh Step prayer helped to anchor my heart in a continual journey of awakening: in ruthless introspection (Step 4), humble confession (Step

5), and surrender to the growth process (Step 6 and Step 7). The final line in the Step 7 prayer—asking God for strength as we go out into the world and serve—could very well encompass the next several steps. In loving service, we need to be accountable (Steps 8 and 9) and continually growing in our awareness (Step 10).

Over time, these prayers have continued to take on new meaning. I'll be honest, though. Some days I pray like I'm on autopilot. Other times a certain word will strike me. That word, *willing*, always seems to challenge me. When I s-l-o-w down and pay attention to each word, it creates almost a forcefield around me as I go about my day. What usually happens if I rush through it a few days in a row, and then I feel my world get wobbly, which makes me return again to my prayer routine. Maybe when we feel out out-of-sync or "off," it's just a reminder that we need to pray. Eventually I start to feel better. The more I'm engaged, the quicker I feel better. This right here might be the most important thing to my sobriety. People ask me how you do it, and this is the thing I did better than anything else. It's not about just doing the prayer to check it off. It's about being present with what's happening and letting God do the rest—and *listening* to God. That's where the magic happens. The fruits of prayer and meditation usually aren't quantifiable, that is, until you're going on your fourth decade of sobriety and reflecting upon your practices that may have helped keep you away from the bottle.

I believe that the Laws of Change begin with self-awareness, with asking questions like, "Where am I?" and "Who am I?" When we can answer those, we can then ask, "What am I doing to get in the way?" And then, finally, we can ask ourselves, "Where do I want to be?" and "Who do I want to be?" In this self-awareness, we are partnering with God to search our hearts. As Psalm 139:23-24 says, "Search me, God, and know my heart; test me and know my anxious thoughts. See if there is any offensive way in me, and lead me in the way everlasting."

It's hard to quantify mindset. It's hard to measure prayer or meditation. But I promise you, it's worth it. Last chapter we talked about maintenance. Prayer and meditation are two things that help position our hearts and minds for continual maintenance; or, in the context of this book, to become more synchronized with the Steps each day. Christian or not, what are you doing to form spiritual rhythm in your own life? What are your practices that help anchor you in a lifestyle of continual change?

❖❖❖

The eleventh step of Celebrate Recovery reads, "We sought through prayer and meditation to improve our conscious contact with God, praying only for knowledge of His will for us and power to carry that out." Again, you can sense some big, powerful words there. *Prayer. Meditation. Conscious contact.* We all long for that conscious contact with our maker. That's a powerful place.

One of the many gifts of Christianity and religion is that, if the beliefs are positive and healthy, they can radically form someone's self-image. It's only through prayer and meditation that we grow to embody these beliefs. Anyone can quote Scripture and come across as smart. Anyone can back up their theology with apologetics—theological defenses of faith. These are worthy pursuits but can be turned into head games. It's through prayer and meditation that our hearts are transformed. That *we* are transformed. That our self-image is transformed into God's image of us. Remember that heart transplant Max Lucado talked about?

In Genesis 1:27, at the very start of the Bible, we read that, "So God created mankind in his own image, in the image of God he created them; male and female he created them." Christianity teaches that when Adam and Eve disobeyed God they became disconnected from God's original intent for them. Shame invaded, as it does for all of us, and they wanted to hide from God. Part of the goal of the Christian life, and the steps as well, is to accept God's vision of who we are and allow love to eradicate shame. Paul lays out the spiritual life in 2 Corinthians 3:18: "And we all, who with unveiled faces contemplate the Lord's glory, are being transformed into his image with ever-increasing glory, which comes from the Lord, who is the Spirit." In other words, as prayer and meditation help us to contemplate God, we too are being *changed* into His image, into who He made us to be. Prayer and meditation anchor us in *keeping* the change because they guide us into a lifestyle of continual transformation. Again, it says 310 times in the New Testament that God loves us. I don't know about you but it's certainly nice to know that I'm loved by God. In knowing that He loves me I'm more capable of loving myself and loving Him. It's tough to love when you're clouded by shame—that cloud slowly dissipating was a big part of the cabin in the woods.

If we don't give ourselves to God, if we're not all-in—giving Him all our character defects (our hurts, habits, hangups, attitude, etc.)—He can't fix it. He'll only fix the things we give to Him. I was free from drugs and alcohol because I gave it to him. For decades I couldn't understand why anger, lust, and insecurity weren't going away. But finally, I gave it to Him.Prayer and meditation help remind me to give it to Him every morning. Every day I remind myself that I am starting fresh. It's like *50 First Dates.* Keeping the change is all about falling in love again and again and again.

Remember Romans 12:2 from the introduction? We are not to be conformed by the world but are to be transformed by the renewal of our minds. So, when it comes to my idols of attention and affection, faith ought to guide me to become more and more aware of how God already fills these needs for me. In awakening to this truth, my idols are slowly deconstructed. They are exposed for what they are: meaningless, a waste of energy, futile. I become less needy, less like a Baby Bart, and become more grounded in God's attention and affection which I must humbly receive, even when I don't feel like I deserve it. Because God has fully loved and accepted me as I am, I don't need to go around chasing affection and attention elsewhere. When that desire to chase things creeps up, that's when I need prayer the most. Prayer is a route that helps us return to our deepest truths. As many spiritual authors have said, prayer is more for us than it is for God.

What if prayer feels empty? What if it feels like there is silence on the other line? That's when we need to trust in values that have served us in the past. When I go to church or work the Steps or pray the Third Step and Seventh Step prayers and don't feel like I "get anything" out of it, that's no excuse for me to search for attention and affection elsewhere. I have to remember how sobriety, discipline, and commitment have changed my life and allowed love to expand in my life.

One of the biblical stories we've been returning to throughout this book is Paul's spiritual journey. Paul may not have been what we would consider an addict, but he certainly had a radical transformation on the Road to Damascus that many addicts also experience in recovery. As we've discussed, he then went through a period of intense confusion, where he was blind and had no idea what awaited him on his journey. And, from thereon out, Paul dedicated himself to continual transformation. He understood that his transformation and his ministry went hand-in-hand.

Just as Paul made the decision that he was going to fight for his transformation, that's what we have to do as well. We have to do the work. We have to *hate* our old behavior. If you still like your old behavior, if you're still attached to your old behavior, change is going to be hard. At the risk of sounding too preachy, consider the following verses. Paul's spiritual wisdom about "loving God with our minds" couldn't be more relevant today as depression and anxiety skyrocket, and as we learn more about the power residing within our minds. Paul, long before our modern developments in neuroscience, often emphasized a mindset change that he found vital to the spiritual life. He was way ahead of his time! Consider these verses:

- "I want to *know* Christ (emphasis mine)," wrote Paul in Philippians 3, "yes, to *know* the *power* of his resurrection and participation in his sufferings." In other words, *knowing* love leads to true power and freedom.
- As he wrote in Philippians 4:8, "Finally, brothers and sisters, whatever is true, whatever is noble, whatever is right, whatever is pure, whatever is lovely, whatever is admirable—if anything is excellent or praiseworthy—*think* about such things." Christian or not, this verse is a good recipe for changing our mindsets, rooted in positivity.
- In 1 Corinthians 14:20, he challenged the church in Corinth, "Brothers and sisters, stop thinking like children (Baby Bart). In regard to evil be infants, but in your thinking be adults." In other words, to follow Christ we must develop our thinking; we must let God form our minds. How might we partner with God in allowing our minds to be formed? In Joseph Grenny's bestselling book *Crucial Conversations,* he talks about nurses in the ER talking to a doctor. They know they have to have adult conversations. If they are lacking self esteem, if they are caught up in some kind of drama, then their patient's life might be at risk.
- Throughout Paul's letters, he writes about "life in the spirit"— this continual abiding in God, this maintenance over our thoughts and actions, that leads to true freedom, true peace. In other words, Step 10 and Step 11 of recovery. And, finally, in 2 Timothy 1:7, Paul encourages us, "For God hath not given us the spirit of fear; but of power, and of love, and of a sound mind

(KJV)." *A sound mind.* Isn't that what we all want? We want peace. We want freedom. We want victory. Step 11 of recovery uses that interesting phrase "conscious contact." In other words, we're aware, present, and connecting with God or our Higher Power as we submit to being continually transformed. I hope this chapter helps equip you to form a sound mind and take control of, what we call in Alcoholics Anonymous, our "stinking thinking."

To make *conscious* contact with what is *true* in this life, whether it be God, your Higher Power, love, or a sense of connectedness, it would help us to gain a simple understanding of our conscious and unconscious mind. Without this understanding, we might think we're making contact with what is true when in reality it's not. It could be a projection of our ego or an emotional idol. Each of us has to grow in awareness of our thoughts. This is all so important. Remember the Matthew Maltz quote? "You can never outperform your own self-image."

Let's dive into this. How do our brains affect our actions? Paul Martinelli once wrote a course called *Self-Image Mastery*, which I'm licensed to teach. In our self-image mastery presentation, we begin by showing the image of a big-headed stickman. Dr. Thurman Fleet designed the stickman, which is a graphic of how the mind works (see figure on the next page). Now, picture a line dividing the stickman's head into two halves. On the top half is the conscious mind, informed by our thoughts (our thinking mind), and on the bottom is our unconscious mind, informed by our *feelings* (our emotional mind). Obviously, we're oversimplifying here to make the brain as practical as possible. Our thoughts impact our feelings, which affect our actions, which lead to either positive or negative results.

DR. THURMAN FLEET'S STICKMAN THEORY

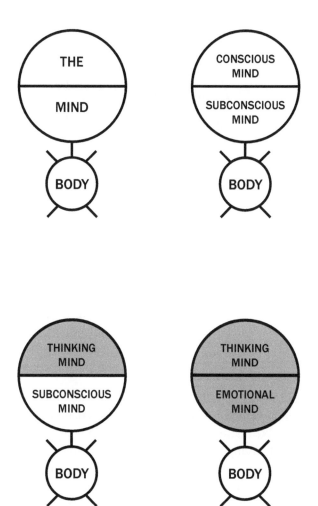

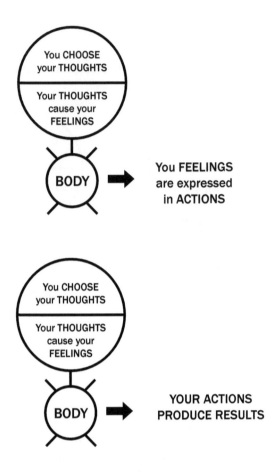

In other words, our *thoughts* affect everything. They are powerful. They form the reality that you subjectively experience. You could be on a beautiful hike that everyone else is thoroughly enjoying, but if your mind keeps focusing on how cold the wind is, that might make you restless or less present, which will affect your enjoyment and conversations, which will affect whether the hike is a positive or negative experience. In addiction, it's often feelings of inferiority and insecurity that might lead an alcoholic to go drink. Drinking makes them feel horrible, which leads them to keep drinking. It's a horrific cycle that begins in the mind, stokes emotional attachment, and leads to terrible results, which fuel the existing insecurity and inferiority, which affects emotion, which leads to more bad decisions, which...you get the point. If your father told you that you were a klutz all the time, that might be why you keep spilling your milk, or beating yourself up for when you spill a small drop of milk.

Ed Mylett once interviewed Trevor Moawad, who talked about his dad being a new-age thinker and a positive thinking expert. Moawad rebelled and said he never bought into his dad's positive thinking theory. Positivity, Moawad said, doesn't always work, but negative thinking *always* works. Negative thinking has four to seven times more power than positive thinking. What does he mean? When we say "I am stupid" or "I can't ever get this addiction cured" those thoughts are eighty percent more powerful. This is why, though I understand why people at recovery meetings introduce themselves with the typical, "Hi, I'm _____, and I'm an alcoholic," I prefer to put this statement in the past tense: "Hi, I'm Bart, and I'm here because I believe in Jesus and have struggled with drug addiction, alcoholism, and sexual integrity in the past." Negative identities breed relapses.

Perhaps you're beginning to see how deep this is. This was likely one of the many reasons why my therapist had me journal about my family every day at the cabin in the woods. He could see that my insecurities were so deeply tied to thought patterns that formed in my youth. His responsibility was to help guide me to the core. My responsibility was to reframe my thinking. Could it be possible that one of the reasons I'd pursue futile, worthless means of affection as an adult was because I felt abandoned as a child? Maybe. No matter, my responsibility was to change how I thought about affection. My parents *did* love me in their own way. They *did* value me in their own way. They *did* care for me in their own way. And, even if I had concluded that they didn't, there *were* others in my life who did. I had to truly make a decision and believe that love I had experienced in the past, love I was experiencing from others now, and God's love for me through it all was enough. If I could change my thinking, I could change my results.

In their book *12 Second Culture* pit crew coaches Mike Metcalf and Shaun Peet share a story about how their racing team experienced several top-five finishes throughout the first half of their season but had some bizarre, unlucky things happen that prevented them from ever finishing first in a NASCAR race. Their racing team was beginning to think they were cursed, doomed to never break through and win. Metcalf and Peet sensed these mentalities and hung up a banner in their team garage that said "WIN OR LEARN." When I heard about this story, I immediately thought of the stickman. They didn't describe it this way in their book, but the banner was designed to change people's *thinking*, to help them transition from a victimized, "we're cursed" mentality to a "win or learn" mentality. Everyone wants to win, but whenever they didn't win, there was so much to learn. Those lessons would inevitably impact their future *results*. The banner helped people realize that there was no negative outcomes. In each lap of each race, they were either winning or learning, never failing. Good story for life, isn't it? We might not be taking laps around the track, but we're going around in life.

What are we going to do to change our thoughts which change our feelings which change our results? Pastor Craig Groeschel wrote a wonderful book called *Winning the War in Your Mind*, an important book today in our mental health crisis that has been caused by the rise of social media and increased isolation with the pandemic. Groeschel writes, "If you want to change your life, you have to change your thinking…We win the war in our minds by creating a solution for our mental ruts: trenches of truth that work with the way our brains work."

It's vital to replace old habits with new habits. Instead of looking for things that you're doing wrong, look for things that you are doing right and repeat them. *I am strong. I am talented.* Consider affirmations that will change the cellular structure of your mind. In the back of Groeschel's book, there are some great affirmations I encourage you to check out. They are really powerful. Here are a few of them:

I am not controlled by fear.
I am not stuck.
I am not a slave to my habits.
I am not a prisoner to my addictions.
I am not a victim.
I am not failing.
I am not unlikable.
I am not unworthy of love.
I am not my past.
I am not what I did.
I am not what someone else did to me.
I am not what others say I am.
I am not who my unhealthy thoughts say I am.

I am not done.

Because of Christ,
I am who God says I am.
I am loved.
I am forgiven.
I am healed.
I am new.
I am redeemed.
I am free.
I am blessed.
I am strong and mighty.
I am Chosen.
I am empowered.
I am a weapon of righteousness in a world of darkness.

Your God is with you.

Now, let's take the stickman to the next level. We show in our presentation that everything that goes into your mind—every interaction, every success or perceived failure—creates a feeling that goes into your *subconscious*. And it's your subconscious that mostly informs your self-image. We drive this point home about the subconscious because the scary thing is that your self-image is being formed even when you don't consciously realize it's being formed. For example, maybe you had an awkward interaction with a good friend. The thought might be, "That was a little awkward," but the *feeling* might be, *I guess our friendship is over, just like so many other failed relationships in my life. I guess I'm just bad at relationships.* As we can see, the feeling is connected to the person's past, fears, ruts, and insecurities. Just as we can reframe our thoughts, we can also reframe our feelings. Not *suppress* our feelings. *Reframe* our feelings. Instead of concluding, *I'm bad at relationships* (based on past rejection) and allowing that negativity to fester and invade our self-image, it'd be better to conclude, *That really hurt when he said that, and I'm going to call him when I've calmed down to sort it out. He's a good friend, and I know we can be honest with each other.*

It's okay to acknowledge how you feel but then ask the question, "What did I learn from that?" If we consistently talk about how much something hurt, we're reliving it over and over again. Take the pumpkin that is your brain, scrape the inside, and fill it with new stuff. Sometimes we're so stored up with the old stuff that new stuff can't come in. We have to empty out. That's the power of therapy. That's the power of a life coach. They help us clean out those pumpkins and fill it with love.

In 2 Corinthians 10:5, Paul encourages his readers to "take captive every thought." Of course, it's impossible to evaluate every single thought that goes into your brain, but mindfulness, prayer, and meditation help us to become aware of *themes* and *trends* in both our thinking and our feeling. The wonderful thing about this is that when you get curious about your thoughts and emotions and commit to reframing them, it yields more healthy actions, which produces more positive results, which then provide *boosts* to your thinking and feeling. See the cycle?

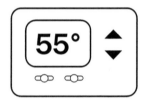

You can almost think of it like a thermostat, HVAC unit, and thermometer. Maybe you have a difficult interaction that sets your inner thermometer at fifty-five degrees. You're feeling down, discouraged, off kilter. You become aware that there is something "off" within you. What is it? Maybe something bad really did happen—maybe your boss took his temper out on you and you know what he did was wrong. Still, your inner dialogue might be making a bad experience even worse. So, you *make a decision* (there it is again), that you want to *change*. You decide to reframe your thoughts and feelings. You decide to take charge and set the thermostat. Changing your thoughts and feelings leads to more proactive (rather than reactive) actions, and, all of a sudden, the temperature of the thermometer begins to rise. Again, none of this happens if you don't pay attention to your thoughts.

This intentional mindfulness helps us make contact with the *truth*. The truth is *not* that you're incompetent because your boss berated you. Maybe it hurt. Maybe you should name how it makes you feel. Maybe you can identify that what he said is reflective of how a loved one once treated you. But now you've named the *lie*. You's exposed it for what it is. And, by exposing it, it has no power over you. The truth is that maybe you made a human mistake (an opportunity to learn), or that your boss becomes a jerk when he's having a bad day. The truth is that you're loved, competent, creative, and have a lot to offer, even though you, yes, sometimes make mistakes. Anchoring yourself in this truth strengthens your self-image. Even more so when you can practice this kind of conscious reframing while in the middle of a storm. Again, we change our thinking about what we want, and because of that, we change our results, which changes our self-image.

Scan the QR code to watch a special message from Bart about Chapter Eleven.

CHAPTER 12
FOUNTAIN OF VALUE

Well, we've made it. We've worked the 12 Steps together. Maybe for a while it felt like you were being emptied by the Steps. As you loosened your grip on your addictions and attachments and deconstructed your notion of attention and affection, maybe it felt like you were slowly being poured out until you had nothing left: of your previous patterns that you thought would fulfill you; of the myths you had long believed; of your past. But hopefully at some point you began to feel like you were being filled up again. That's the thing—we can't be filled with what is spiritually true in this life if we are constantly filling ourselves with what is false.

For twenty years I had no capacity for spiritual truth because I filled my soul with my addiction. Recovery felt like I was being emptied. Humility can feel that way, can't it? Sobriety made space for prayer, and the deeper patterns in my life were exposed for what they were: as unhealthy, as selfish, as destructive. My addiction to alcohol and drugs had only masked the deeper patterns that ran my life.

I realized I had to be emptied yet again. Once more, I had to *admit* I was powerless, *believe* I could be restored, and *make a decision* to turn the pattern over to God. I had to continue to work the Steps with humility as my guide. I had to let God fill me with spiritual truth: a new way of living. The more I was emptied of each pattern revolving around a false sense of attention and affection, the more capacity I had to be filled by something *real*, something *true*. Love. Freedom. Christ.

Peace. And the more I was filled by spiritual truth that nourished my body, soul, and spirit, the more these truths overflowed onto others. Into parenting. Into being a husband. Into leadership.

The other day someone asked me which step I was working on, and I struggled to answer him. Yes, there are some days when a particular step reveals itself to me, but most weeks I'm working through all of them throughout the day. My life has become fused with the Steps. The Steps permeate my being and my days. God changed me through them and continues to do so today. The Steps are my spiritual rhythm that continue to make me into a new creation (2 Corinthians 5:17).

The twelfth step of Celebrate Recovery reads, "Having had a spiritual experience as the result of these steps, we try to carry this message to others and to practice these principles in all our affairs." If we authentically engage the Steps, we'll be empowered to, as John Maxwell says, lead people in a way where people of value are adding value to people of value. What does this mean? We are all loved by God. The truest part of who we are is love. Each of us contains infinite value in God's eyes. If we can't accept this truth, then our own pride and arrogance is likely blocking us from receiving unconditional love. We truly *are* people of value, surrounded by others who have infinite value. Each of us has the great opportunity to love, serve, and lead each other in a way that helps those around us to uncover more of their inherent value. This is the key to significance.

One thing I've learned through working the steps is that this step summarizes it all, but it's also who I am today. Today I'm a husband, a teacher, a mentor, a coach, a speaker. In Step 12, we take that spiritual experience of hanging out with God everyday and overflow onto others.

The key to significance is to give, give, give, and give some more. It's not about what's in it for me—it's about what's in it for *we*. If we go back to Maxwell's Five Levels of Leadership, Pinnacle (the final level) is when you have leaders developing leaders. This is what the twelfth step encourages us to do: use what we've experienced on our own journey through the Steps to help others. Our deep introspective journey through the Steps helps us better understand ourselves and the human condition. This helps us to better understand others and have empathy for them in their own flaws and shortcomings. In being emptied of our patterns and old ways, we can help others, too, experience life anew. In gaining deeper humility on our journey, we can love and serve others more fully, which hopefully creates a culture of more people doing the same. AA says that you can't keep what you don't give away. In my podcast, Keep the Change, I interview people who have worked through their brokenness and are now adding massive significance in other people's lives. The goal of the podcast is not only for listeners to hear about my guests' victories but also to learn from their breaking points.

When I ashamedly picked up the phone nearly forty years ago and called the Adrian Center, I had no idea what was in store. I thought I'd get help for my cocaine addiction and would go on drinking and partying after I was released. God obviously had something else in mind. I embraced a life of sobriety. I went all-in. Deeper patterns were exposed. I found God in the walls of a church (and outside the church). I went to years of therapy. I spent thirty days in the woods. There were times when the introspective journey was excruciating, when shame showed its face again, when my past tempted me with self-contempt. But overall, there's been victory. There's been peace. Boundless hope. Love that I didn't even know was possible.

We've been emptied. We've been filled. Now it's time to overflow. I'll end this book with the question that began this book: *What is it you would like to change?* I hope the Steps help you to *keep* the change—to adopt a lifestyle of continual transformation. I hope the peace and victory and freedom you experience along the way helps inspire you to keep changing. One of the greatest gifts God has given us is the opportunity to constantly grow.

By the way, your journey might not be my journey, but your journey to God is the most important journey there is. You don't have to go in the woods, but there are certain things you have to do to get to freedom on the other side. You can do this. I might not know you, but you got to the last page of this book. That's commitment. Put that same effort into one day, one hour at a time, and your life will change. I want to congratulate you in advance. You are loved.

Scan the QR code to watch a special message from Bart about Chapter Twelve.

STEP 1: We admitted we were powerless over our addictions and compulsive behaviors and our lives had become unmanageable.

STEP 2: We came to believe that a power greater than ourselves could restore us to sanity.

STEP 3: We made a decision to turn our lives and our wills over to the care of God.

STEP 4: We made a searching and fearless moral inventory of ourselves.

STEP 5: We admitted to God, to ourselves and to another human being the exact nature of our wrongs.

STEP 6: We were entirely ready to have God remove all these defects of character.

STEP 7: We humbly asked Him to remove all our shortcomings.

STEP 8: We made a list of all persons we had harmed and became willing to make amends to them all.

STEP 9: We made direct amends to such people whenever possible, except when to do so would injure them or others.

STEP 10: We continued to take personal inventory, and when we were wrong, promptly admitted it.

STEP 11: We sought through prayer and medication to improve our conscious contact with God, praying only for knowledge of His will for us and the power to carry that out.

STEP 12: Having had a spiritual experience as the result of these steps, we try to carry this message to others and practice these principles in all our affairs.

---

*Steps to recovery as originated by Alcoholics Anonymous and reintroduced by Celebrate Recovery with Christ as the Higher Power.

RESOURCES

Half Time
Bob Buford

Love Works
Joel Manby

The Success Principles
Jack Canfield

Extreme Winning
Pat Williams

The 15 Laws of Growth
John Maxwell

*Everyone Communicates,
Few Connect*
John Maxwell

*Developing the Leader
Within You*
John Maxwell

The 5 Levels of Leadership
John Maxwell

Winning the War in Your Mind
Craig Groeschel

Self Image Mastery Course
Paul Martinelli

Think and Grow Rich
Napoleon Hill

12 Second Culture
Mike Metcalf and Shaun Peet

*Alcoholics Anonymous:
The Big Book*
Bill W.

Celebrate Recovery
John Baker

*The Greatest Salesman
in the World*
Og Mandino

Start with Why
Simon Sinek

The Secret Society of Success
Tim Schurrer

The Ruthless Elimination of Hurry
John Mark Comer

Just Like Jesus
Max Lucado

BOOK BART TO SPEAK AT YOUR BUSINESS, CHURCH OR ORGANIZATION

Topics include:

Leadership | Personal Development
Mental Health | Sales | Recovery
Celebrate Recovery | Alcoholics Anonymous
Parenting | Goal Setting | Marriage Recovery
Walking with Jesus in Recovery
Massive Change | Communication
Self-Image Mastery

bart@bartnollenberger.com

GET YOUR
DISC ASSESSMENT

$100 Disc Assessment, including a **FREE** half-hour coaching session with Bart

Sign up today!
bart@bartnollenberger.com

LEADERSHIP COACHING FOR YOUR GROUP, CHURCH, OR ORGANIZATION

10-week intensive Manager Bootcamps on topics by John Maxwell including:

- Developing the Leader Within You 2.0
- The 15 Invaluable Laws of Growth
- Everyone Communicates, Few Connect
- Leadership Gold
- The 21 Irrefutable Laws of Leadership

In addition:

Other Leadership Bootcamps

- Think and Grow Rich
- Self-Image Mastery

Sales People and Managers

- Sales Masterclass Bootcamp

bart@bartnollenberger.com

KEEP THE CHANGE

Keep the Change Podcast
available on

 Apple Podcasts

 Spotify Podcasts